"Randy Hemphill is a man who has e
powerful ways, and he knows how to lead
will find *The Restored Man* to be an importa
a tool to help others in their unique journeys. The insights in this book are biblical,
practical, and transformational."

—Dr. Mark Searby, director, Center for Pastoral Resilience

"A man's journey and strength is vital to the family and the local church. In *The
Restored Man*, Randy Hemphill provides men with a process for growth with God
and others. And it works! I would encourage pastors and churches to use this
resource."

—Johnny Hunt, senior pastor, First Baptist Woodstock,
former president of the Southern Baptist Convention

"Dr. Randy Hemphill understands that God brings lasting change to men from
the inside out. *The Restored Man* offers a process that digs down deep into the soul
of a man, exposing sins and the idols of a man's heart. I have found *The Restored
Man* to be an excellent resource for men who desire real change and practical
encouragement in becoming men of God."

—Buddy Gray, pastor, Hunter Street Baptist

"Attend one of Randy's speaking engagements and you get exactly what this book
delivers: effortless honesty and exceptional guidance. It's time for you to 'check-in'
with Randy (and other brothers) and become an authentic man in Christ!"

—Jim Barnette, professor of religion, Samford University

"If you are tired of living life behind the shiny paint of your exterior while secretly
deteriorating on the inside, I urge you to encounter *The Restored Man*. You will
never be the same."

—Dr. Robert Smith Jr., Charles T. Carter Baptist Chair of Divinity,
Beeson Divinity School, Samford University

"We cannot afford to look at men as problems that need fixing nor as projects
that need to be managed. In *The Restored Man*, Randy Hemphill comes alongside
the reader as a fellow traveler and experienced guide. He sweeps aside the quick
fixes and invites us on a journey of spiritual and emotional maturity. This soul-
searching process is worth every moment of the journey."

—Doug Webster, professor of pastoral theology,
Beeson Divinity School, Samford University

"The world needs restored men. Randy Hemphill has walked this journey personally and now offers you the opportunity to do the same. His personal experience of living from a restored heart makes *The Restored Man* a must-read for men who want to live fully alive."

—Dale Forehand, founder, Stained Glass Ministries and author of
Often Told, Rarely Trained: Becoming the Man You've Always Been Told to Be

"*The Restored Man* invites the reader into a journey of spiritual transformation. Those who accept this invitation will discover that God is ready to restore them to His original intention."

—Brian Lee, senior pastor, Shades Crest Baptist

"Both restoring a car and restoring a life takes a slow process. That process is clearly defined in *The Restored Man*. In this book you will discover tremendous ways to begin this process to a restored life, a restored marriage, and a restored hope!"

—Mark Harrison, executive pastor, Gardendale First Baptist Church

"Randy Hemphill takes you on a relatable journey through his personal experience on how to become a restored man. His profound wisdom and encouraging story of rebuilding a car will surely impact and change the heart of any man who reads it. Anyone who accepts the challenge of this process will find it has amazing benefits in both their personal and married life."

—Alan Worley, president and CEO, Money Pages

"Randy Hemphill not only shows us where we should be but he underscores *how* we can get there. It can be frustrating to be reminded of what we are not and what we should be without the tools and processes to experience change and growth. Thanks, Randy, for showing us how to step into and embrace the foundational pathways to growth and spiritual maturity."

—Dr. Crawford W. Loritts Jr., author, speaker, radio host, and
senior pastor, Fellowship Bible Church

"*The Restored Man* is a must-read for men truly desiring to find freedom from the traps of dysfunctional manhood and be ever more formed in the image of Jesus."

—Dr. Nathan Joyce, senior preaching pastor, Heartland Church

"For well over a decade I've watched Randy Hemphill walk side by side with men to help them restore their marriages, deal with their pasts, and find a closer walk with Christ. It takes hard work, and not everyone is ready for it. But if you are, you'll be blessed to invite him into your journey."

—Adam Robinson, senior pastor, Double Oak Community Church

"Take the items in *The Restored Man,* use them to dive deep into the community of brotherhood, and unleash your masculinity in the circle of folks you have and who has you."

—Paul Johnson, LMFT, LPC, NCC, LifePractical Counseling

"Wherever you are as a man—single or married, have/had a great or poor relationship with your dad—Randy Hemphill's *The Restored Man* will touch your heart. It will challenge, encourage, and biblically remind you how much the Lord wants to father you. I recommend this book to any man who desires to be the man God wants him to be. Restoration is yours for the taking!"

—Rodney Wilson, pastoral counselor, LifePoint Church

"In *The Restored Man,* Randy Hemphill is a straight shooter who displays courage as he casts both practical and spiritual wisdom for becoming the man God intended you to be. Are you ready to be restored? I strongly encourage you to lock in on this book—with a humble heart and open mind!"

—Eric Frye, president, Waynes Environmental Services

Other books by Randy Hemphill

30 Days of Hope for Hurting Marriages (with Melody Hemphill)

THE
RESTORED
MAN

Becoming a Man of God

R ANDY H EMPHILL

An imprint of Iron Stream Media
Birmingham, Alabama

Iron Stream Books
5184 Caldwell Mill Rd.
St. 204-221
Hoover, AL 35244
NewHopePublishers.com
IronStreamMedia.com
New Hope® Publishers and Iron Stream Books are imprints of Iron Stream Media.

Iron Stream Media serves its authors as they express their views, which may not express the views of the publisher.

Library of Congress Cataloging-in-Publication Data

Names: Hemphill, Randy, 1974- author.
Title: The restored man : becoming a man of God / Randy Hemphill.
Description: First [edition]. | Birmingham : New Hope Publishers, 2018.
Identifiers: LCCN 2018043740 | ISBN 9781563094705 (permabind)
Subjects: LCSH: Men--Religious life--Textbooks.
Classification: LCC BV4528.2 .H454 2018 | DDC 248.8/42--dc23
LC record available at https://lccn.loc.gov/2018043740

Additional resources can be found at www.therestoredman.com.

ISBN-13: 978-1-56309-470-5

Printed in the United States of America.

1 2 3 4 5—23 22 21 20 19

They will be called oaks of righteousness, a planting of the LORD for the display of his splendor. They will *rebuild* the ancient ruins and *restore* the places long devastated; they will *renew* the ruined cities that have been devastated for generations.

—Isaiah 61:3–4 (emphasis added)

A process . . .

A guide . . .

A brotherhood . . .

A restoration of your masculine heart!

Reverend Carl Hemphill . . .
Dad . . . you're the richest man I know . . .
this one's for you!

CONTENTS

Writing, like restoring an old car, is a long and messy process. Even if you do most of the work on your own, you rely on the wisdom and direction of others. No person writes or rebuilds alone. It takes a community of trusted, faithful individuals. May I share a few of those who joined me in the process of writing this book?

Allies of LIFE Ministries . . . you have faithfully supported us over the years. Thank you for undergirding the work and enabling Melody and me to minister to many.

Restored Man Pit Crew . . . brothers, you prayed for me and gave much needed feedback during the writing process. From allowing me to share writer's block to personal struggles, you listened and loved me well over the months.

Friends at Iron Stream Media . . . you have gifted me with an opportunity to fight for men's hearts through writing.

Dad . . . your heart is in these pages. My story hinges on your story. This book's for you!

Mom . . . you believed before I could. Thanks for seeing and knowing my heart.

Ty, Rich, and Brett . . . my true band of brothers. Glad we get to live this together.

Max and Frank . . . the use of your cabins for writing provided the perfect spot for soul-rest and soul-writing.

Caleb, Brennan, and Asher . . . I'm far from the perfect dad, but I pray my life mirrors some of the truths in these pages. I love you and am proud of you.

Addilyn . . . Oh, how you melt this daddy's heart. I hope I've modeled masculinity and our Father's good heart for you.

Melody . . . there are no words to match my love, respect, and honor for you. Best friend, fellow minister, lover, and daughter of God . . . you'll always have my heart.

Finally, to the men who have entrusted their stories and hearts to me over the years. You have modeled brokenness and vulnerability. Thank you for allowing me to step into your journey and learn together about the fathering heart of God.

Soli Deo Gloria . . . Glory and honor to our good Father!

MEN, SOMETHING IS MISSING

Tucked behind Grandpa's homeplace there's an old barn. It's been sitting there for years. Beaten by the sun and weathered with time, it sits and even sags. Tinkering around in Grandpa's backyard, you walk over and peer through the slats of old wood.

Particles of dust float through the air and dance through the traces of sunlight. Looking around, there is everything from old tools to greasy buckets. A leaning workbench sits on one side and is topped with Maxwell House coffee cans, each filled with rusty screws and an assortment of washers, nuts, and bolts. Over to your left, you see something hidden in the back. Draped with a cloth, tucked away from the light, something calls you from the dark corner.

You decide to walk in. Barn doors are always hard to open. They stick from years of harsh winters and dry summers. You pry the homemade lock and pull hard on the door. It opens and welcomes you with a musty, dark aroma. Walking in, you maneuver around piles of newspapers, a disassembled tractor, and a stack of dusty tires.

You meander to the covered item. What could it be? Pulling back the thick blankets, your eyes widen at the sight of an old race car.

The barn door creaks. "Son . . . what are you doing out here?"

"Hey, Grandpa. Oh, I was just looking around at some of your stuff. Wow, you have some real treasures out here."

"Well," Grandpa says, "I don't know about treasures . . . just a bunch of old memories that I can't seem to part with. I see you found Daisy."

"Oh, so that's what you call her? Daisy?"

Grandpa moves a few steps closer, "Yes, Daisy. Built her back in the day. Took a few years . . . only put her on the tracks a couple times. She's a beauty, isn't she?"

You stammer with your words, "You mean . . . you . . . put this . . . I mean built this by yourself?"

"Yeah," Grandpa throws his hand over your shoulder, staring, "Spent a lot of time in the garage. I've got some drawings over there on the workbench, under those coffee cans. Those sketches were dreams that eventually turned into this."

"I just can't believe you never showed this to me. This is . . ." you stammer for words . . . "unbelievable!"

"You know," your grandfather mutters, "she needs some work done. Been sitting here for years. That last race was a mess . . . she never recovered."

"So, you just brought the car back here?"

"Yeah, parked her back here. Doubt she even runs. I'm just too old to mess with it."

He shuffles his feet a bit, staring out the cobweb-filled corner window.

"You know, kind of odd you came out here today. I was just reminiscing about Daisy and how much I would love to hear that engine hum again."

"Grandpa," you say, "do you think . . . I mean . . . could we maybe work on this together?"

"You mean restore ol' Daisy?" he says.

"Yeah, you and me. We could do this together. You guide and give me instructions. I'll do the work," heart pounding, "and we could make this our project."

"You know, son," Grandpa looks you in the eyes, "that's a wonderful idea. I'd love to spend time with you, and I'd love to see this beauty back on the road."

With that, a relationship sparks, a rebuild commences, and a restoration takes place.

His name was Coffee, and he was our tour guide for the day. This caffeinated caretaker matched the age of the vintage vehicles at the Barber Vintage Motorsports Museum. Located just outside Birmingham, Alabama, this museum is a storehouse of breathtaking motorcycles, cars, race cars, and other vehicles that have been restored. I am not a car or motorcycle enthusiast, but the idea of a Restoration Tour caught my eye.

I signed up and arrived at the museum around nine. As a small group waited, I ended up in a conversation with an older gentleman from Canada who bestowed some race car knowledge from many years spent on the tracks. Though car and engine lingo were secondhand to him, I was mostly lost as he talked about body styles and engine types. But his short stories of race cars and old dirt tracks were mesmerizing.

A few minutes later, a voice called from the lobby where we had wandered off from, "If you signed up for the Restoration Tour, we are ready to begin." I shuffled over with the group of fifteen or so and noticed our tour guide's name tag . . . Coffee. That's when I knew this gray-haired, wiry fellow was going to be perfect for our tour. Who doesn't love a name like that?

Our lively tour commenced with stories that ranged from how the museum was created to how the collection of cars and motorcycles was acquired. Five levels of breathtaking vehicles in vintage condition. In fact, Coffee said the majority of the vehicles in the museum are operational. Wish I could have taken a ride in the '57 Chevy or one of the old Harleys.

We finally arrived at the bottom level of the museum, what is referred to as the Restoration Level. This is the area where specialist mechanics work each day to carefully tear down and restore vintage motorcycles and vehicles. It was amazingly clean and well organized. Coffee said most restoration projects take months to years to complete.

Each restoration is worked through with a fine-toothed comb to ensure every part has the exact look of the original. When they can locate original parts, they travel the world to acquire them. When unavailable, the artists/mechanics work to recreate the original.

This part of the tour fascinated me. I asked some questions of the mechanics and got "behind the counter" to see the tools, parts, and work involved in such an art. I wondered, "What must it be like to spend months or years carefully handling such a rare find? How many hours would be spent on one restoration project? And was it worth it?" Most of my questions were answered by the simple look in the eye of the rebuilder. Yes, all the hours, sweat, and work were worth it to behold the finished product.

THE PROCESS OF RESTORATION

There are many books and Bible studies that have been written for men over the years to help us grow in relationship with God. I have read and worked through many of them. But, over the years, I must admit that there is a glaring weakness, a missing piece, to most men's books and resources. The missing piece is *process*. I hear men say it often, "I know who I shouldn't be . . . I know who I should be . . . but how do I get there?"

I have found three major imbalances or weaknesses in men's resources.

Behavior over heart.

Whether it's the latest Bible study or a Father's Day sermon, our tendency is to harp on the unhealthy and unfit behaviors of men. You might even hear the words, "Man Up!" Now guys, let's be honest . . . a lot of this is deserved. We have helped create a culture of angry men and passive men. Whether the behavior is explosive and violent or passive and indifferent, we have not always behaved well. So, let's own it. But instead of coming up with another "Top 10 behaviors every man needs to work on" list, let's go after the heart. Let's do something that is going to last longer than a few weeks or months.

To change a man's behavior, we must go after something much deeper. We must go after his heart . . . your heart . . . my heart. *The Restored Man* is not another get-it-together checklist or a set of religious practices to prop you up for another year. Instead, the following chapters will provide a process to restore your broken, masculine heart. You'll hear this in a bit, but it is worth saying now . . . God does not want to fix you but to father you. Behavior matters but only as it flows from a restored heart.

Points over process.

As a man, there is a natural tendency to treat this book as a business plan for masculinity. Like attending the latest workshop or conference for your job, we leave with loads of information, a stuffed three-ring binder, and maybe a nice pen with the company name on it. Is there a need to gain knowledge? Yes, the phases of *The Restored Man* will hopefully enhance your knowledge of Scripture along with your understanding of the masculine journey. But please do not stop at knowledge and information. I want this book to be practical. More than making some great points and filling in the blanks, let's enter in to a process. God is not inviting you to another conference or workshop to make some points, hand you a binder, and get you in line. He is your Father more than your boss or CEO. God is inviting you into a process.

Spiritual over emotional.

When you hear the word *spiritual*, what comes to mind? Maybe church, Bible, prayer, accountability, and worship make the list.

When you hear the word *emotional*, what comes to mind? Maybe weak or unstable . . . some might even say feminine. Here's the point: Most men's resources attempt to tackle the spiritual issues while neglecting emotional growth. I must admit that God has opened a whole new world for me in seeing growth as both spiritual and emotional. Pete Scazzero, though I have never met him, has been a mentor in this area. One of his lines has stuck with me: It's impossible to be spiritually mature while remaining emotionally immature.[1] That line is worth reading a few times. If we are going to grow as men, our growth will be both spiritual and emotional. For example, your relationship with God, in some way, is influenced by your relationship with your dad (see phase 1: Know God as Father). Exploring your story, friendships, sexuality, relationships, and heartaches will enhance your connection with God (see phase 2: Know Self). Exhibiting brokenness and humility is both a spiritual and an emotional practice leading to a deeper life with God and others (see phase 3: Live in Brokenness and Humility). Disciplines such as prayer, Bible study, accountability, and warfare are avenues for God to grow us spiritually and emotionally (see phase 4: Walk with God in the Disciplines).

Instead of placing the spiritual above the emotional or vice versa, *The Restored Man* lays out a process that balances the two. There's that word again: *Process*. Brothers, it is the missing piece. More than correcting behaviors, making some points, or enacting some religious practices, God is inviting you . . . inviting me . . . into a process of restoration. Are you ready to get started?

---

[1] See *Emotionally Healthy Spirituality* by Pete Scazzero and visit emotionallyhealthy.org.

Chapter 1

STARTING POINT: WHY DO THIS?

"Whew . . . sure is dusty in here." Grandpa props open the flimsy barn doors. "Haven't had these open in quite a while."

Tossing the blankets to the side, your voice echoes from the back of the barn, "So, we're pushing this up to your garage? Throw it in neutral, and I'll push from behind. We'll eventually get ol' Daisy up there." It was taking you a while to get used to calling a race car Daisy. Seemed oddly personal to call a car by name. But you went along with it.

"Now, hold on just a second," Grandpa says with some force. "We need to clear out a path first before we can roll it out. In fact, grab those two buckets over there. Yeah, the two stacked in the corner." You grab the buckets, handing them to him. Grandpa pulls the buckets apart, flips them over, and sets them on the ground.

"I know you're ready to get things started but I've got something to ask you." A bit bewildered you take a seat. Seems odd to sit down when you are chomping at the bit to get this car up to Grandpa's garage. "Ok . . . um . . . sure, Grandpa. What's on your mind?"

"Well, actually, that is what I'd like to know . . . What's on your mind? You know, before we get this whole restoring Daisy process going, I'd love to know why. Why do you want to do this?"

Tilting your head with a confused look, "Why do I want to do this? Grandpa, I'm not sure what you're asking. I just thought we were going to get your old race car running again."

"Well, it is important to know the why before we tackle the what. Sure, we are going to spend a lot of time tearing down and rebuilding Daisy. I'll walk you through it. But I'd like to know why you want to do this. What do you hope to accomplish beyond fixing a car?"

1

Staring back out the cobweb-filled window in the corner, a piercing silence settles in the barn. A gentle breeze whirls through the open doors and glides across your face. Your eyes travel down from the corner window and make a final stop at the dusty, barn floor.

"You know, Grandpa, when you mentioned working on this car together, something came alive in me. I mean, I've never worked on a car or built anything." You turn your right shoe sideways and shuffle dirt back and forth while talking. "But now that I think about it. I guess I just want to spend some time with you."

Grandpa's crossed arms open up, and he leans in, "Son, thank you. That's what I wanted to hear. Getting the car fixed up is a great goal for us. It'll take us some time, a lot of effort, and a good bit of patience. But I want you to know," Grandpa's voice quivers as he places his hand on your shoulder, "the time with you is what really matters."

Most men do not like to ask for directions. I can recall several road trips with the family where this truth prevailed. We would launch out on a family vacation or holiday trip. I had a general feel for where we were going and how to get there. Please remember, this was before the time of Google Maps or GPS. "Who needs a map?" I would say. I have a built-in directional system that knows how to get to the right place. The problem was my system had plenty of faulty programming that I chose to overlook.

I remember one trip where we were travelling up north. I believe we were somewhere in Indiana. There was an accident ahead on the interstate, and the police had created a detour to avoid congestion. Most drivers were taking the marked exit and following the vehicle in front. But me? No, I wanted to create my own detour. Well, it was a detour all right. A detour that ended up adding several hours to an already long trip.

At some point in my self-created detour, I realized I was lost. My wife Melody was helping the kids, fixing snacks, and doing the normal crowd control in our minivan. She was honestly oblivious to the lost state we were in. And then I faced the dilemma. I'm on some weird, back road in Indiana, late at night with screaming kids and absolutely no idea where I was. Do I admit my failure? That seemed almost like heresy. Or do I keep driving into the eternal abyss of flat-road Indiana?

At one point, Melody leaned over and said, "Do you know where we are?" I responded, "Ummm . . . I thought we were . . . I kept looking for this sign . . . I . . . yeah, I don't know . . . we are lost." We pulled over, regrouped, backtracked a bit and finally saw a rest area in the distance. With great relief, I steered the minivan into the rest area, threw it in park, and took a deep breath. I walked up to the rest area lobby and found the map. And there were the words I was waiting to see . . . YOU ARE HERE. Finally, I could begin to get a plan. It required admitting my confusion and even failure. And it required getting a starting point, a you-are-here moment.

Men need starting points to provide direction. A baseline forces us to pause, assess where we are, and then determine next steps. Before we start walking through the four phases of restoration, it is important to do some self-evaluation. Don't skip this step . . . trust me, the payoff will be great down the road.

AN EXERCISE IN DESIRE[2]

We begin with desire because Jesus begins with desire.

In John 7:37, Jesus made a bold and loud statement on the final day of the Feast of Tabernacles, "Let anyone who is thirsty come

---

[2]For a fuller treatment of desire in the Christian life, see James Houston's *The Heart's Desire: A Guide to Personal Fulfilment* (1992) or John Eldredge's *Desire: The Journey We Must Take to Find the Life God Offers* (2007).

to me and drink." To understand the weight of this statement, we must understand the feast in which Jesus was speaking. The Feast of Tabernacles was one of three pilgrimage festivals the Jews celebrated (the other two being Passover and Pentecost). During the Feast of Tabernacles (or Booths), there were two important images: booths and water. The booths were the temporary dwellings the Jews built to live in for a period of seven days to remind them of the years of wandering in the wilderness when the children of Israel relied on God's provision (see Exodus 20–40).

The second important image was water. Each day, priests would carry water from the pool of Siloam and pour it on the altar. For this culture, water was life. They were dependent on water for crops and livestock. Water on the altar represented their dependence on God and His provision. On the seventh and final day of the feast, the priests would carry water, walk around the altar seven times, and then pour the water on the altar. It was on this day, the culmination of the grand festival, when Jesus made the bold statement in a loud voice, "If anyone is thirsty, let him come to me and drink." Now that was a revolutionary statement.

In the chapters preceding this bold statement, we have the stories of Jesus' interaction with thirsty people. By thirsty, I mean people who were soul thirsty. They were hungry or thirsty for something that would satisfy. Think of thirst as desire. When a person is thirsty, he or she is longing for something. To be thirsty is to have a deep desire for something more. And, as we will see, Jesus tapped into desire.

We begin in John 3 with Nicodemus, trapped in religion but longing for something more. Nicodemus went to Jesus at night (v. 2), which signifies some type of embarrassment. Being a religious man, Nicodemus knew the cost of a conversation with Jesus. His Pharisaical credentials could be called into question if his conversation with Jesus was brought into the light. They had a late-night conversation that centered on desire. I like to imagine them sitting around a campfire, a great place for men to open up.

Nicodemus had noticed something different about Jesus and the way He interacted with people. Jesus' loving and heart-addressing message stood in contrast to the harsh and behavior-centered message of the religious. Nicodemus asked questions, and Jesus conversed with him. They discussed being born again, but don't miss Jesus' method of dealing with Nicodemus' heart. After reading the story (vv. 1–21), notice how Jesus basically asked, "Why do this?" or, "What do you want?" To deal with desire is to deal with the heart. Jesus' invitation to a relationship of love and light cuts against the grain of religion. Maybe you can connect with Nicodemus's story. How has religion and going through the motions of trying harder and managing the externals worked for you? Do you want something more?

Whereas Nicodemus went in the night, the Samaritan woman in John 4 went to the well in the middle of the day, the hottest time of the day. This would be the time of day when the well would have been vacant of people. Why? She was filled with shame and was probably a woman with a "label." It was likely most people in the town knew her story and her struggles. As the story reveals, she had been married five times and was living with a sixth man (v. 18). Relationships were obviously not satisfying her thirst.

Jesus, a Jew and outsider to the Samaritans, walked up to this woman at a place of water and asked her for a drink. This interaction led to a conversation about thirst, water, life, and worship. Jesus basically said, "I know your life and your story. I know you have looked to relationships to quench your thirst. That does not seem to be working out so well. What do you want? Do you long for something that will truly and eternally satisfy your soul's thirst?"

Now, that's my version of what happened. Read it for yourself. Jesus does not defy or deny desire. Instead, he taps into it. What are you thirsty for? What do you want?

It was religion for Nicodemus. It was relationship for this woman. Both are toxic when used to gain identity and value. As a man, how have you used religion to prop yourself up? How have you used relationships with women or sexual gratification to find validation? How's that working for you?

And finally, in John 5, Jesus approached a man at a pool. Once again, the image of water springs off the pages of Scripture. This man had been an invalid for thirty-eight years. For nearly four decades, someone had been dropping this man off periodically at a pool that supposedly had magical powers and would bring healing. Certainly, the man had grown hopeless over the years. His condition had become his identity.

Jesus walked up to him and asked a simple question, "Do you want to get well?" Let that question sink in. Here's a man who was clearly in need of a miracle. Jesus knew his story and knew his need (see John 2:25). And yet Jesus still posed the question, "Do you want to get well?" What was at play here? Jesus was tapping into desire. He was asking this man a question like he asked Nicodemus and the woman at the well . . . "What do you want? Do you long for something more? What are you thirsty for?" Jesus always had and still has a way of cutting straight to the heart.

Religion for Nicodemus . . . relationships for the woman at the well . . . and circumstances for the man at the pool. Each had lost hope over the years and decided to settle for circumstances that were killing their hearts. Makes me think of the line, "Maybe this is as good as it gets." Killing desire kills a man's heart. How have you shut off your heart? How have you killed desire? And how have you lost hope by settling in your circumstances?

Jesus is interested in your heart and in your desires. Far more than a behavioral program or an external washing, Jesus wants to restore and redeem your masculine heart. He came to bring life. And He begins here . . . with desire. So what do you want? Take some time to answer the following questions. No need to rush. Meditate on the questions, and then jot down some thoughts concerning your desires.

SURVEY

Personal

What do you want in your relationship with God?

How do you want to grow emotionally in the coming months? (How you want to progress in the way you handle anger, depression, sadness, fear, etc.)

When you see yourself in five years, what do you hope to see? What do you want that man to be like?

Marriage and/or Relationships

What do you want in a relationship with your wife or future wife?

Define a healthy marriage.

What does a spiritually and emotionally healthy husband look like?

What does a spiritually and emotionally healthy wife look like?

If married: When you see your marriage in five years, what do you hope to see? What do you want the marriage to look like?

Self-Assessment[3]

The restoration process will involve four central phases. To provide a starting point or baseline, fill out the following self-assessment.

Respond to each of the following statements by writing a number next to each statement that best represents your experience. It is best to answer according to what reflects your experience rather than what you think your experience should be. Give the answer that comes to mind first. Do not overthink questions.

SURVEY

Phase 1: Know God as Father (Write a number between 1 and 5 for each of the following statements, 1 being not true of you at all and 5 being a definitive truth of your life.)

I feel confident in my relationship with God. _____

I am frequently aware of God prompting me to do something. _____

I enjoy worshipping God by myself as well as with others. _____

I am closely connected with a community of other believers. _____

---

[3]I relied on two resources for the creation of this assessment. Peter Scazzero, *The Emotionally Healthy Church* (2015) and Peter C. Hill and Ralph W. Hood Jr., editors, *Measures of Religiosity* (1999). Digital versions of assessments can be found at www.therestoredman.com.

I have spent time exploring my relationship with my earthly father and learning how this affects my relationship with my heavenly Father. _____

Total Score: _____

What is the first image that comes to mind when you think of God?

Briefly describe your current relationship with God.

Phase 2: Know Self (Write a number between 1 and 5 for each of the following statements, 1 being not true of you at all and 5 being a definitive truth of your life.)

I am willing to explore emotionally unhealthy issues in my family of origin. _____

I am comfortable expressing emotions like anger, sadness, fear, and loneliness. _____

I openly admit my losses and disappointments. _____

I do *not* need the approval or validation of others to feel good about myself. _____

I am able to resolve conflict in a respectful and timely manner. _____

Total Score: _____

Briefly explain your lowest score from Phase 2 or give an example.

Phase 3: Live in Brokenness and Humility (Write a number between 1 and 5 for each of the following statements, 1 being not true of you at all and 5 being a definitive truth of your life.)

I am able to admit wrongdoing and ask for forgiveness. _____

Family members or close friends would describe me as approachable and a good listener. _____

I am able to speak openly about my weaknesses and mistakes. _____

I receive criticism as constructive and have a teachable spirit. _____

It is rare that I judge or belittle others. _____

Total Score: _____

Briefly describe your ability to be transparent and vulnerable in relationships.

Phase 4: Walk with God in the Disciplines (Write a number between 1 and 5 for each statement below, 1 being not true of you at all and 5 being a definitive truth of your life.)

I carve out regular times in my schedule to be alone with God. _____

Reading the Bible and prayer are a regular part of my daily activity. _____

Hearing from God is a consistent part of my Christian journey. _____

I know when my "spiritual tank" is low and make time to feed my soul. _____

Family members or close friends would say I balance work and family well. _____

Total Score: _____

How have you viewed the word *discipline* in relation to the Christian life?

Total score for all four sections (out of 100): _____

Which section was your lowest score?

Wife/Friend Assessment

For this section and to provide additional feedback, ask your wife or a friend to fill this out. Compare and contrast this assessment with your self-assessment. As we begin this process, these assessments form a baseline for your personal growth.

Instruct your wife or close friend that this assessment is their opinion or perspective of your current spiritual and emotional state. Their answers will assist you in this journey with God and with them.

Instructions:

Respond to each of the following statements by writing a number in the blank that best represents your perspective of your husband's/friend's experience. It is best to answer according to what reflects your experience rather than what you think it should be. Give the answer that comes to mind first. Do not overthink questions.

SURVEY

Phase 1: Know God as Father (Write a number between 1 and 5 for each of the following statements, 1 being not true of the person being assessed at all and 5 being a definitive truth of their life.)

He feels confident in his relationship with God. _____

He is frequently aware of God prompting him to do something. _____

He enjoys worshipping God by himself as well as with others. _____

He is closely connected with a community of other believers. _____

He has spent time exploring the relationship with his earthly father and learning how this affects the relationship with his heavenly Father. _____

Total Score: _____

Briefly explain your lowest score from Phase 1 or give an example.

Phase 2: Know Self (Write a number between 1 and 5 for each of the following statements, 1 being not true of the person being assessed at all and 5 being a definitive truth of their life.)

He is willing to explore emotionally unhealthy issues in his family of origin. _____

He is comfortable expressing emotions like anger, sadness, fear, and loneliness. _____

He openly admits his losses and disappointments. _____

He does *not* need the approval or validation of others to feel good about himself. _____

He is able to resolve conflict in a respectful and timely manner. _____

Total Score: _____

Briefly explain your lowest score from Phase 2 or give an example.

Phase 3: Live in Brokenness (Write a number between 1 and 5 for each of the following statements, 1 being not true of the person being assessed at all and 5 being a definitive truth of their life.)

He is able to admit wrongdoing and ask for forgiveness. _____

Family members or close friends would describe him as approachable and a good listener. _____

He is able to speak openly about his weaknesses and mistakes. _____

He receives criticism as constructive and has a teachable spirit. _____

It is rare that he judges or belittles others. _____

Total Score: _____

Briefly describe his ability to be transparent/vulnerable in relationships.

Phase 4: Walk with God in the Disciplines (Write a number between 1 and 5 for each of the following statements, 1 being not true of the person being assessed at all and 5 being a definitive truth of their life.)

He carves out regular times in his schedule to be alone with God. _____

Reading the Bible and prayer are a regular part of his daily activity. _____

Hearing from God is a consistent part of his Christian journey. _____

He knows when his "spiritual tank" is low and makes time to feed his soul. _____

Family members or close friends would say he balances work and family well. _____

Total Score: _____

Briefly explain your lowest score from Phase 4 or give an example.

Total score for all four sections (out of 100): _____

Which section, of the four, was your lowest score?

Chapter 2

KNOW GOD AS FATHER

"You know, your dad always loved cars . . . maybe a little too much," Grandpa *says as he slowly gets up from being perched on the bucket. Walking over to Daisy, the old race car that now sits uncovered, waiting to be moved, he says, "There are some things you need to know about your dad. Never knew when the right time would be."*

Still sitting on the bucket, you chime in abruptly, "Oh, I'm fine, Grandpa. I've tried not to think about him over the years. I mean, I was only eight. I've managed pretty well on my own."

Turning toward Daisy and gliding his hand across the hood, Grandpa collects his thoughts. "I know it was a long time ago. I guess you were about eight. And yes, you have managed quite well. But, son, I need you to listen closely to me. A father/son relationship . . . well, it's a mighty important one."

"But Grandpa," your voice a bit shaky, "when Dad left, I was young, and I just thought that was normal. I mean, Mom did the best she could to raise us. And me . . . well, I just learned to do life on my own. I never knew that I missed anything."

"I know, but you did miss out . . . on a lot of things. You see, your dad was really into cars; probably because I was into cars. Sons seem to have this built-in longing to connect with their dads. Guess you could say God put it there. And cars were our thing. We could spend hours working on an old race car and never say a word. It was our space, I guess, to connect. But to be honest, I did not do the best job of connecting with him. And before I knew it, time had slipped away. Cars gave way to . . . well, a lot of other things."

"Wow, so you and my dad worked on cars? Kind of like we're about to . . ."

Grandpa interrupts, "Yes, but we never talked like you and I are talking right now. To be honest, son, I didn't know how to handle this father/son stuff. I taught him a trade but didn't know how to teach him about life and struggles and relationships." Dropping his head and staring at the dusty, barn floor, he says, "I guess that's part of why he left. He eventually started drinking a bit too much. Your mom, well, after they married, she hoped it would go away. Who doesn't? And then we slowly drifted apart."

Grandpa's eyes shift back to the cobweb-filled window in the corner, "And then came the night your dad left. Your mom called me, hoping I could come over and talk him out of it. He'd had a few too many drinks that night, his anger got the best of him, and as he was leaving . . ." A tear glides down Grandpa's cheek and settles on the dusty floor. "Your dad screamed, 'I'll never come back.' And he didn't . . . he left."

Slowly rising from your bucket seat and moving toward your grandfather you say, "So that's what happened. I remember staring out of my bedroom window. I had no idea. The only thing I knew was that Dad left. I remember watching you run after his truck, but I guess it was too late. And I guess that's the day that everything changed for me."

Grandpa pulls you close, wrapping his long arm around you, "Sure did . . . a lot changed that day . . . for you and for me. Tough on a daddy's heart and tough on a son's heart. But you . . . I am so proud of the man you have become. And, son . . ." placing his hands on your shoulders, "listen closely to me. Sometimes a man must go back to go forward. Just like ol' Daisy will have to be broken down to be rebuilt, so goes a man's life." Squaring his shoulders, head cocked to the side, he adds, "But hey, we'll have plenty of time to talk about that. For now, let's roll Daisy up to the garage."

There was once a man who had two sons.

—Luke 15:11 *The Message*

Nearly all the wisdom we possess, that is to say, true and sound wisdom, consists of two parts: the knowledge of God and of ourselves.

—John Calvin, *John Calvin: Writings on Pastoral Piety,*
edited and with translations by Elsie Anne McKee

THE CABIN RETREAT

It was a holy moment . . . a moment where time stood still.

My father, Carl Hemphill, and I found ourselves in a cabin nestled in the mountains of Sevierville, Tennessee. It was planned as a father/son outing. Several weeks prior, I had approached my dad about going on a trip together to "pass on the blessing." He was approaching the sage years of life, and I sensed the need to spend some extra time with him. Passing on the blessing, though I had no clue what it would look like, came from a desire for validation from my earthly father.

We spent a lot of time talking and reminiscing. We revisited parts of our stories that we had either never mentioned or rarely mentioned. It was like spending time with a best friend who knew you on the deepest levels. We ate some great food. I remember the night we set out to find the best steak and ribs. We landed at a place and enjoyed the manly delicacies of steak, ribs, potatoes, and sweet tea. We were stuffed. But I remember my heart being hungry for so much more.

The cabin had a hot tub on the back porch that provided a nightly visit for us to relax and reminisce some more. We laughed, we cried, and we created memories that get stored deep in the heart of a man.

On one night, Dad pulled out a journal he had been writing in and shared some parts of his own journey. His writings provided a window into his soul and his journey of fatherlessness. You see, my dad never had a dad. He had a man who functioned in the role of father but who never grew into Dad. My dad grew up in parts of Michigan and Indiana. His father was a truck driver. Life on the road brought its fair share of wild living and chasing dreams. My grandfather, whom I barely knew, spent his life chasing sunsets and never found the light. And my dad's mom? She carried her own pain and found escape through the use of alcohol, dying around the age of forty. This spilled over into the family life where my dad and his siblings got passed around from one family member to another.

My dad's MO (modus operandi) and way of surviving was to do life on his own. It is truly the greatest tragedy of fatherlessness . . . to believe you are on your own. But my father had to survive and create his own path. Leaving high school early, he joined the US Marine Corps in search of a father figure. He received tastes of that through the stern, demanding voices of sergeants and captains in the military. But the void remained, and my dad functioned on his own.

Life on our own is a tragic way to function as a man. In fact, it cuts against the grain of faith that says God is dependable and trustworthy as a heavenly Father. Fatherlessness or unfinished fathering breeds mistrust, doubt, fear, and anger in a son. A son is left to pick up the pieces of his anger and grief while blazing a manmade trail for himself. It is an epidemic of our culture that leaves every man injured and some men impaired for life.

My dad eventually married my mother, his high school sweetheart, and they began a life together. Three sons later, on a hot night in Florida with a flaming evangelist, God melted my dad's heart, and his God journey began. His faith beginnings were certainly not the most ideal. Less like a father and more like a judge, God functioned as the "god with a big stick" in his life. Legalism would trump grace. And law would overpower love. It worked for a long time

I was born just a short time later, followed by a call from God for my dad to enter full-time ministry. My parents packed up, went off to Bible college, and did the impossible. They journeyed through college in their thirties with four kids and limited resources. It is a story to tell that will have to fill the pages of another book. Miracle after miracle paved the way for a lifetime of faithful ministry to God. The gospel continued to be preached in the best way possible, and people's lives were transformed through this pastor, my dad.

As I sat with my dad at our mountain retreat and he read from the pages of his journal, the voice and heart of a hurting man could be heard. It was filled with the "beat the hell out of you" verses that get twisted to produce slaves, not sons. It was the voice of my dad's earthly father framing the voice of his heavenly Father—angry, absent, and apathetic. That was the God my dad had known. His heart was complete and secure in Christ, yet there was a gaping hole, a fatherless void.

My dad's story is every man's story. It is a long, hard journey of trying to make life happen and functioning on our own. My story unfolded in completely different ways with fewer heartaches and neglect. My dad was and is an incredible dad. But he is human, an imperfect reflection of the true Father. I had needs too, and I longed for a deeper connection with God and with my dad. I craved validation, the kind of validation only a perfect, good, faithful Father can provide.

Earthly fathers are unable to provide that in its fullest form. And they were never intended to. God created man with a father void inside. You might call it "father hunger."[4] We are born in a broken world, a fallen world. Call it original sin. I prefer to call it "original fatherlessness." We are born with a need and desire for validation. It is the kind of validation that can only come from a father. Earthly

---

[4]Term borrowed from Robert S. McGee's *Father Hunger* (2015).

dads are meant to meet some of those needs while paving the way for relationship with God. The most ideal path for a son is when relating to and trusting God flows out of relating to and trusting Dad. Imperfect fathers who embrace brokenness and lean on God continually create that kind of culture for a son (or daughter). Imperfect fathers can point to a perfect Father.

Your story may be more like my dad's story, a fatherless story. A journey filled with deep and direct father wounds. These are wounds that impair a child and make trusting God seem impossible. Whether your dad was physically absent or emotionally disconnected, he left you on your own. He left you abandoned. Maybe he was abusive in some way. Maybe he cheated on your mom. Maybe he berated you with his words or gestures. Maybe he treated you more like a piece of furniture than a human being. Those are direct wounds that leave a man stranded on the side of life's road.

Your story may have more similarities to mine. Instead of an absent or angry dad, you grew up with a solid foundation. You have positive and warm memories of your earthly father. Though imperfect, you felt cherished and treasured by him. Maybe he was your biggest fan on the field, on the platform, or on a stage. As good as the relationship might have been, your dad was still imperfect. Indirect wounds and hurts still take place. Maybe your dad was often "there but not there." He might have hidden behind the newspaper or television. His work may have drained his energies with little reserve for you. He may have dealt with hurt or instability with your mom that sapped his fathering strength. Divorce may have even entered the picture. Just because your dad was a "good man" does not make him a perfect man. He had flaws, and he fathered with those flaws. These result in indirect father wounds. They can be more difficult to identify.

Most sons with "good dads," with stories more like mine, find it difficult to identify the fatherless elements in their stories. To even talk about father wounds or hurts sounds like a betrayal of trust. It removes dad from the pedestal of hero and places him on the pavement of humanity. And that honest removal or journey feels like betrayal. The goal is never to paint your dad in a bad light or blame him. Blame gets us nowhere. Your journey with God, though, requires honesty and brokenness. It requires that you look honestly at your father-son relationship, admit the broken places and hurtful absences, and declare dependence on the only perfect Father . . . that is God, the Father to the fatherless.

Whether direct or indirect, father wounds cripple a man and impair his ability to function in life and in relationship with God. Anger seeps out of every son's heart and fuels our passivity, destructive behaviors, and ineptness in relationships. There are fatherless places in every man. At the core, we are unfathered to various degrees and left with a deep ache for validation. Every man craves validation and looks to a multitude of things and people to satisfy that hunger. Ultimately, only God can satisfy the desire for validation. Only the perfect Father can give you identity and life. He gave you the desire and only He can satisfy it.

On the final night of our mountain retreat, my dad and I decided that it was time to pass on the blessing. Neither of us had a clue as to what that meant. We only knew God created the space and time for us to encounter something special. The details of how this blessing would be accomplished were unknown, which created some anxiety. But we stayed present to God's plan and trusted His provision with the details.

Earlier that day, while going through his luggage and clothes, my dad found a small bottle of anointing oil. Years ago, a friend had visited the Holy Land and brought my dad back this small container of oil (I guess oil from Israel must be more "holy" than regular oil). To this day, my dad has no recollection of placing the container in his luggage. It had been in his dresser for years. We were card-carrying

Southern Baptists. Anointing was something that took place at the charismatic church down the road, the "holy rollers." My dad had stashed this bottle in the dark corner of his dresser so no one in the church would ever think he had gone charismatic or something. Somehow, this small vial of oil made it into his luggage. It was an angelic and prophetic move on Someone's part.

That night, my dad came out of his room, told me the story of the anointing oil, and said he would like to anoint me and pass on the blessing. Moving over to the rustic couch in this mountain cabin, my dad took a seat. I kneeled and placed my face at my father's knees. With tears streaming down his face, my father began to pray over me and anoint me with oil. Though the exact words or phrases are hard to remember, I recall the holiness of this moment like few in my life. It marked me as a son and grounded me as a man. My heavenly Father validated me through the heart of my earthly father.

And what happened next would take this moment and make it a marker . . . for my dad and for me. In humility, my dad said, "You know, Randy, I never had much of a dad. I never received a blessing like this. Would you do me the honor of passing on a blessing to me?" And that's when time stood still. That is when the little cabin became a sanctuary. We were on holy ground. I responded, "Dad, I would be honored and humbled to do that." And what happened next is hard for me to describe in human words. I sat on the couch and my dad kneeled. Placing his head at my knees, I began to pray and began to anoint. My tears anointed him far more than the holy oil (You can't buy that in the Holy Land). Once again, I have no recollection of the words or phrases that were shared. But I remember the moment. A blessing, a validation, was given by the Heavenly Father through the heart of a son. And time stood still.

Before we move on, take a moment to write a few responses to the previous story.

What struck you most about the story of my anointing experience with my dad?

What is your primary emotional response after reading the story? (celebration, sadness, anger, confusion, doubt, etc.)

Have you ever connected validation with fathering? Describe the connection in your own words.

How did you receive validation from your earthly father?

In what ways did you miss validation from your earthly father?

The result of being unfathered or partially fathered can result in anger. This anger fuels a lot of our addictions, behaviors, and relational struggles. What have you done with your anger? How has it shown up in life and relationships?

At this point in the journey, what is your response to seeing and relating to God as Father? (hopeful, hesitant, questioning, anxious, etc.)

BREAKING IT DOWN: YOUR FATHER

The next section is going to require your head and your heart. It is going to require some focused time and attention. If you are in a rush, feel free to put the book down and return at a better time. Block out some time, get alone with God, and walk through the following questions. These questions will help you explore your relationship with your father, his personality and character, and the effect he has had on your life.

It is important to answer based on your childhood and adolescent years. It may be helpful to answer some questions based on your years in elementary school, middle school, and high school.

When you hear the word *dad* or *father*, what is your initial response? What is the primary emotion you feel when you think of *dad*? (fear, sadness, anger, gladness, frustration, apathy, etc.)

What did you call your father? (Dad, Pop, Daddy?)

What are the first five words that come to mind when describing your father?

How did your father deal with anger?

How often did you see your father cry? How did he grieve?

How did he treat your mother, his mother, or other women?

How did your father handle faith and relationship with God?

Did your father talk with you about sex? How did he handle sexual topics with you or other family members?

Did your father communicate the words, "I love you," or, "I am proud of you"? How often?

Were there any significant events involving your father? Describe their effect on you. (divorce, job loss, financial difficulty, affairs, addictions, death, etc.)

Describe a time when you felt a strong, emotional connection with your father.

How affectionate was your dad?

Rate your father on the following scale. Where would he fall in each category?[5]

Respects Opposite Gender   Has Contempt for Opposite Gender

| 1 | 2 | 3 | 4 | 5 | 6 | 7 | 8 | 9 | 10 |

Intimate   Emotionally Distant

| 1 | 2 | 3 | 4 | 5 | 6 | 7 | 8 | 9 | 10 |

Sacrificial   Selfish

| 1 | 2 | 3 | 4 | 5 | 6 | 7 | 8 | 9 | 10 |

Truthful   Hypocritical

| 1 | 2 | 3 | 4 | 5 | 6 | 7 | 8 | 9 | 10 |

Consistent   "Anything Goes" Mentality

| 1 | 2 | 3 | 4 | 5 | 6 | 7 | 8 | 9 | 10 |

Communicative   Secretive

| 1 | 2 | 3 | 4 | 5 | 6 | 7 | 8 | 9 | 10 |

---

[5]Adapted from Robert S. McGee, *Father Hunger* (Ann Arbor: Servant Publications, 1993), 67–79.

Responsible								Assigns Blame	
1	2	3	4	5	6	7	8	9	10

Instills Self-Confidence								Instills Guilt	
1	2	3	4	5	6	7	8	9	10

With all your reflections about your father, what effect has he had on your life? (In positive and/or negative ways.)

How is your view of God and relationship with God *similar to* or *different from* your relationship with your earthly father?

Are you willing to admit the lens through which you see God is somewhat blurred by human relationships and experiences . . . including your relationship with your earthly father?

OK, we may need to take a short breather after the last exercise. Spending time reflecting on your relationship with your dad can be exhausting, in good and in difficult ways. It can stir a lot of emotion. Some emotion stems from happy memories of spending time with your father and feeling validated as a son. Other emotion surfaces from the hurt, pain, or loss you have experienced in this vital relationship. It may have stirred some anger you have not felt in a while. No matter the emotional response, you are choosing the right path of delving into the father-son relationship. Do not feel like you must rush ahead to the next section. If needed, let the previous pages soak before moving on. Be honest with God, and ask Him to meet you in these moments and speak to your heart.

BUILDING UP: THE PRODIGAL'S FATHER

All of Scripture is inspired and needed to understand God. We spend a lifetime diving into the whole Bible to get a complete picture of a holy and loving God. That is the essence of theology. Theology is not some nice, technical word for seminary-trained Bible students. No, theology is the way we think about and relate to God. Everyone has a theology and is developing a theology. Whether you realize it or not and whether you've taken a class on the Bible or not, you have a theology. You have a way of thinking about God and relating to God.

By exploring our relationships with our earthly fathers, we are revealing the lens through which we see God. Our relationship with our fathers is a primary lens in a man's life, in a son's journey. Because our earthly fathers are human, prone to sin, and imperfect, the lens blurs how we see God. If your dad was distant and uninvolved, you may tend to think of God the same way. If your father was angry or abusive, you may think of God in terms of being strictly wrathful and stern. If your dad was affectionate and present, it may be easier to draw close to God. The father lens is important in every man's life. But because the lens is either shattered or blurred, we must replace it with the truth of God revealed in the Bible. We must come to know God on His terms instead of on our terms, our experiences, and our lenses for life.

For a few thousand years, the church has studied and meditated on Luke 15, the parable of the prodigal son. This story is primary to shaping the lens through which we see and relate to God as Father.

In verses 1 and 2, we find the context for Jesus' telling of the parable. Jesus had created a following of broken people. Tax collectors and sinners were drawn to Jesus and His teachings. There was also a group called the Pharisees. They were the religious gatekeepers of the day. Their desire was to honor God and to protect the law. Now before we jump on the "Pharisees are horrible people" bandwagon, we must understand that these were not grumpy, old men looking for a fight. They were authentic, on some level, in their desires and calling. Though religious, their intentions were to protect what they thought was right. In their attempts to uphold truth, they discounted the very reason for the law's existence.

Jesus told three stories in Luke 15 to an audience of sinners and religious people. Both were present in the circle of listeners. I am guessing the tax collectors and sinners were probably pressing in as Jesus told the stories while the Pharisees listened from the outskirts. Broken people tend to be more open to seeing the faulty lenses through which they see God. Religious people, like the Pharisees, tend to be reluctant to admit their faults and blurred vision.

How are you like the tax collectors and sinners?

How are you like the Pharisees, the religious?

The Parable of the Lost Sheep

Read Luke 15:3–7, and answer the following questions.

In your own words, describe the story.

What does this story reveal about God?

Verse 7 is the main point of the story. Write it in your own words.

Verse 7 compares repentance to self-righteousness. To repent is to admit your "lostness" and brokenness. It involves spiritual and emotional honesty. It involves humility. Self-righteousness does just the opposite. Why is repentance so important to a relationship with God?

Parable of the Lost Coin

Read Luke 15:8–10, and answer the following questions.

In your own words, describe the story.

What does this story reveal about God?

Verse 10 is the main point of the story. Write it in your own words.

Repentance or brokenness is once again highlighted as central to relationship with God. Everything within a person fights against repentance. As men, it feels weak to admit we are broken. To admit failure seems to unravel our masculinity instead of build it up.

How do you struggle with admitting brokenness?

What does pride look like in your life?

Repentance can be a "churchy" word. How does this story give you a new lens for seeing repentance and brokenness?

Parable of the Lost Son

Read Luke 15:11–32, and answer the following questions.

The younger son asked for his share of the estate. This would have been equated with wishing death upon your father and family. This was a serious request. What does it reveal about the younger brother's heart?

Verse 17 contains a pivotal statement, "When he came to his senses." The younger brother arrived at the point of brokenness. An awakening took place in him that ultimately led him to journey home. What does it mean to "come to your senses"?

Verse 20 may be one of the most powerful and potent verses in the Bible. Take a moment and write the verse below.

Now personalize the verse by writing it again, this time with your name and "my father" inserted.

What does verse 20 reveal about God as Father?

Is this the God you have known?

Are you willing to see God through the lens of this parable, the Parable of the Loving Father?

In verse 21, how did the younger son own his sin?

Describe the celebration that took place in verses 22–24.

The story continues with the older brother in verses 25–32. What is he angry about?

The father pleaded with him; yet, what was the son's response?

The story ends with an unanswered question. Jesus does not tell us what happened to the older brother. Do you think this was intentional on Jesus' part? How do you think the story ended?

How does Luke 15 impact the way that you see yourself?

How does Luke 15 impact the way that you see God and relate to God as Father?

Chapter 3

KNOW SELF

"Whew, that was a lot of work!" said Grandpa as Daisy was rolled into the garage. "I had forgotten how far it was from the barn to the garage. That's quite a trek. Thanks for your help, son."

"No, problem, Grandpa . . . I can't wait to get started on this rebuilding project. Who knows? Old Daisy may get to revisit her glory days and . . ."

Grandpa interrupts, "Oh, sorry son, I completely forgot to get the paperwork in the barn. We'll need that. Would you mind running back down there? Over to the right, on my bench is a set of papers. If I remember right, it's under one of those Maxwell House coffee cans."

Nearly sprinting, you jot out the garage door and head back down to the barn. You remember seeing a stack of papers on the workbench, grease-stained and weathered. Arriving at the barn, you immediately head in and to the right. Grandpa's workbench. You wonder how many hours he spent sitting at this table, pondering over these papers. Lifting the coffee can, you pick them up. Hmmm . . . you think to yourself, some of these seem like blueprints. Filled with straight lines, part details, and lots of numbers. But underneath those is a stack of random, handwritten notes. Several pages of Grandpa's notes. Must have been edits or changes he was making during the building process.

"Here you go, Grandpa." Returning to the garage, you hand the papers to him. "Hope you don't mind, but I looked over the papers. Seems like a mixture of blueprints and a bunch of notes. Why do we need these?"

"Ah, quite inquisitive, aren't you? Well, son, we will definitely need these to restore this old race car." Flipping through the stack of papers, "I spent many

hours drawing up the blueprints for Daisy. In my mind, I knew exactly what she would look like and how she would run on the racetrack, but I had to draw it out on paper. These will be handy to get Daisy back to her original design."

"Oh, I see. But what about this other stack of notes?" Pointing to the papers with greasy fingerprints and torn edges, "I can tell these are your handwriting, but why do we need these? They seem a bit jumbled and messy."

"Seems like I spent as many hours, or more, making these notes and edits while building Daisy. Things never go as planned. In the process of building, I had to make several changes based on what worked and what didn't work. Trust me, we'll need these too."

"You know, Grandpa, all of this car building sure has me doing a lot of thinking. You were just talking about my dad . . . your son . . . which got me thinking about my story. Things I haven't considered in a long time." Pointing at the blueprints in Grandpa's left hand, "Guess you could say there were some blueprints drawn up for my life too."

Grandpa responded, "That's right, son. And here," holding up his right hand filled with the messy stack of papers, "are the pages of edits, changes in your story. A man's life is always being shaped through experiences, struggles, and hurts. And a wise man will spend plenty of time studying pages like these."

Laying the papers on the driver's seat, Grandpa stares at Daisy and then looks over toward you, "And speaking of struggles, let me tell you one about Daisy . . ."

GOD made my life complete when I placed all the pieces before him.

—Psalm 18:20 *The Message*

Story is the primary way in which the revelation of God is given
to us.

—Eugene H. Peterson, *Leap Over a Wall:*
Earthy Spirituality for Everyday Christians[6]

People look at the outward appearance, but the LORD looks at the
heart.

—1 Samuel 16:7

TWO AFFAIRS . . . ONE BROKEN MARRIAGE

Every man has a story. And every man's life is telling a story.

I can still remember the words flowing from her heart as she sat
on the cedar chest at the end of our bed . . . "I'm just not in love with
you anymore." It was December 2003, and our marriage had been
dying a slow death for years.

Melody and I met in our first year at Campbell University,
home of the fighting camels (how's that for a mascot?). We met on
a Baptist Student Union (BSU) retreat where the goal was to get
away and spend quality time with God. Somewhere between my
morning devotion and the scheduled time of worship, I had a "road
to Damascus" experience where I was blinded by love. Melody says
it began as a friendship. I remember it differently. Before online
dating and matchmaking services, there was the BSU retreat. Even
card-carrying, toe-the-line Baptists cannot prevent the divine and
romantic work of the Holy Spirit.

A short time after meeting at the retreat we began dating. I will
never forget the conversation that took place late one night at the
soccer fields of Campbell. We were parked in my 1981 Ford Courier.
It was a real beauty with rusty fenders, a leaky A/C unit, and a motor

---

[6]Peterson's book on the life of David is one of the best at unfolding the
details of the David story. I relied on Peterson for structure and flow of
this chapter.

that could be heard in the adjacent town. We had been talking for hours when suddenly one of us said, "Are you thinking what I'm thinking? You know . . . maybe . . . um . . . marriage?" We knew God had brought us together, and we were most certainly in love. A few years later, in the summer of 1995, we were walking the aisle at Melody's home church to begin married life. We were so "in love" at the blissful, young age of twenty.

The early years of marriage were filled with ministry, school, and a few moves. We wound up on the outskirts of Birmingham, Alabama, serving a church while I pursued a degree at Beeson Divinity School (located on the campus of Samford University). Those were busy months filled with study, work, paying bills, and trying to figure out married life. We were miles away from family, and though it forced us to lean on each other, it also created an inner loneliness.

I eventually finished school and went on staff at a church in Birmingham. Neither of us realized how much our relationship operated on fumes and how much baggage we had brought into marriage. I continued to pour into work and climb the ladder of validation through career. All the while, our marriage was dying.

When Melody breathed the words, "I am not in love with you anymore," it was a declaration that our marriage was at a crossroads. I knew it. She knew it. The youthful love had disappeared, and it seemed as though divorce was inevitable.

It was during this time that two affairs were revealed. Melody's was with another man . . . a two- to three-year relationship that had developed in darkness and secrecy. My affair was with work, being seduced into thinking my identity would improve through my job. And on that lonely night in December, everything was exposed.[7]

---

[7]To learn more about mine and Melody's story, and to strengthen your marriage, see my book *30 Days of Hope for Hurting Marriages.*

The next several mornings, I remember waking up and looking in the mirror for what seemed like an eternity. I stared at myself and wondered, "How could this happen . . . to us? Who are you? What have you become?" I was confused, hurt, and empty. Have you ever had an experience like that where you felt lost? An experience where you realized your life as a man had become buried in career, success, and relationships? These are the crossroads of a man's life. We encounter them at various stages in the masculine journey. They are seasons filled with loneliness, doubt, fear, and even despair. Questions like "Who am I?" "What is my life about?" "What's my purpose?" and "What kind of man have I become?" fill the air. Crossroads like these can feel suffocating and deflating.

In the previous chapter, we laid the foundation of knowing God as Father. We now turn to knowing self. These two truths, know God and know self, are interdependent. They are inseparable. John Calvin, one of the great reformers and pastors in church history, once said true wisdom is found in the knowledge of God and of ourselves. He put it like this: "The knowledge of ourselves not only arouses us to seek God, but also, as it were, leads us by the hand to find Him."[8] Leads us by the hand . . . what an image! The journey of knowing self and knowing your story functions as a guide to knowing God. We are not talking about self-help or self-discovery as much as God-help and God-discovery. Every man must take the journey of knowing self if he is to know God.

So that's what I did. I began a journey of understanding Randy Hemphill. It has been the most challenging and fruitful season of my life. It exposed my deepest hurts and fears. It forced me to explore my inadequacies in relationships . . . fear of conflict, approval

---

[8]John Calvin, *John Calvin: Writings on Pastoral Piety*, ed. and trans. Elsie Anne McKee (New York: Paulist Press, 2001), 68.

addiction, inability to express anger, low self-esteem, struggles with depression, and pride, to name just a few. It emptied me yet filled me. I faced the dark corners of my heart yet never experienced such light. I knew the god I had created but now have come to know the God who created me. It is the process of restoration, the rebuilding of broken men. And that's me . . . broken and being restored in Christ. It is the path I will continue to take. Restored while always in process of being restored to God, my Father.

The following pages are going to be like whitewater rafting. I will function as your guide leading you through the waters of your story and your life. We are going to utilize God's Word, specifically the story of King David in the Old Testament, to unpack a man's story and to unpack your story.

In the pages of the Bible, there is more written about David than any other human character. Sixty-two chapters of the Old Testament are committed to David's life while no less than fifty-nine references in the New Testament call attention to him.[9] We meet young David the shepherd in 1 Samuel 16, and later in 1 Kings 2, this king is laid to rest. Seventy years of life that proved to be filled with defeat and victory, sin and life, betrayal and romance, adultery and murder, and tears of grief and tears of relief. The details are unique, but David's story is every man's story. Let's take some time to look at David's life and relate each part to our journey as men. Put on your life vest and helmet, grab an oar, jump in the raft, and let's see where the Holy Spirit leads us.

KNOW YOUR BEGINNINGS (1 SAMUEL 16)

When we meet David in 1 Samuel 16, things were not well in Israel. Saul, Israel's first king, consistently wavered between pleasing people and pleasing God. Eventually, the prophet Samuel delivered some

---

[9]Charles R. Swindoll, *David: A Man of Passion and Destiny*, (Dallas: Word Publishing Inc., 1997), 195.

strong words to King Saul: "You have rejected the word of the LORD, and the LORD has rejected you as king over Israel" (1 Samuel 15:26), and chapter 15 ends with the sobering statement, "And the LORD regretted that he had made Saul king over Israel" (v. 35). And now the stage is set for a new king.

Samuel, the prophet of God, went into the town of Bethlehem on a mission to anoint the next king of Israel and Judah. Upon arriving in Bethlehem and making peace with the authorities, Samuel sought out Jesse and his sons. God had told him the next king would be found in this house. The only problem was Jesse had eight sons to choose from.

Boys play pick-up games all the time. Whether dodgeball, baseball, or football, team captains are chosen, and then there is the infamous "draft." Captains look over the varied bunch of boys and then make their choices. And how do you know who to pick? Well, you go after the biggest and best first. One by one, players are drafted based on their apparent skill set and size. It was the backyard combine before the NFL ever created it. And then, toward the end, one boy would remain. The runt of the bunch. The last man standing. Rather than being chosen, the remaining captain would mutter, "Alright, Johnny, I guess you're on our team."

Choosing David to be the next king went something like that. All his older brothers were displayed before Samuel. The big hitters and defensive ends took the stage. Then the best outfielder and running back were paraded before this agent of God. With each one, to Samuel's surprise, God said no, so Samuel said no. Tryouts were over and still no king. Samuel must have wondered, "Well, am I at the right house? Is this Jesse's ranch or did my camel GPS send me to the wrong place?" He must have scratched his head and said, "Um, Jesse, I'm a bit confused; you got any other sons?" Jesse sat bewildered, looked around, and then reluctantly said, "There's the youngest, but he's out taking care of the sheep. I guess we could go get him."

Remember our last chapter on knowing God as Father? Here is a perfect example of a father wound. David is called "the youngest." He is not even referred to by name but only by position in the family (the youngest) or title (shepherd). To be overlooked by a father is to be wounded by a father. The role of a father is to bless, affirm, and validate. It is to bestow identity. David, the kid brother, is overlooked by his earthly dad and devalued as a son.

The servants ran out to the field and called David to the house. *What did I do this time?* Young David approached the house, kicked off his sandals, and propped his shepherd staff against the front door. He entered the family room with a cloud of dust and the scent of sheep. And immediately God said, "This is the one." While a mere teenager, David was anointed as the next king. Wounded by an earthly father yet chosen by his Heavenly Father. The beginnings of a great story.

Where were you born?

What's the first memory you have of growing up?

Did you have a nickname?

Did your family move or stay in one place?

What was your first job?

Describe your favorite elementary school teacher.

Do you remember your first "crush" on a girl? Do you remember her name?

As a boy, what were some of your favorite games to play? Sports? Adventures?

Did you have a favorite superhero? Who?

Boyhood is meant to be filled with adventure, fun, freedom, and wildness. Would you describe your boyhood that way? If not, how would you describe it?

Thinking about the early years of your life. Did you experience any hurts, betrayals, or losses? Jot down any that come to mind.

KNOW YOUR BATTLES (1 SAMUEL 17)

After being anointed by Samuel as the next king, David goes back to tending sheep. At this point, only God, Samuel, and a handful of family members even know of the plan for David to be king. So David goes back to his day job. At the same time, the Spirit of God has departed from King Saul, and an evil spirit from God is tormenting him (1 Samuel 16:14). Saul's heart was given over to pride, and he elevates his kingdom over God's kingdom. David gets called up one day to go and play the harp in Saul's palace. The music from young David functioned as a temporary antidepressant for King Saul. David's melodies on the harp soothed Saul's anguishing, angry heart. How ironic . . . God's tunes were being played during Saul's internal battle with evil. We are introduced to David the warrior and David the musician. What a combination!

We now come to 1 Samuel 17, one of the most famous scenes in David's story. It is a battle scene. If you've been in Sunday school or church for long, you have heard the story of David and Goliath. It's certainly a familiar story to me, and one I like to imagine in great detail. On one hill, the mighty Philistines were taunting and breathing fire against God's people. On the other hill there was Saul's army filled with fear and dismay. In between, there was a valley with a heavyweight battle in the works.

David goes back and forth from Saul's palace to the sheep fields. First shift took place in the fields, tending to the sheep. Then, he would race to his second shift job where he would clean up, take out the harp, and play tunes for the king. One day, he overheard talk of this giant, Goliath, who was taunting God's people. This giant stood over nine feet tall and was outfitted in the best armor of the day. No need to exaggerate this giant's credentials. He truly stood head and shoulders, and another head and shoulders, above the rest.

David heard the news and wound up in Saul's oval office for a meeting. David declared, "Let me fight this uncircumcised Philistine." Saul's response was similar to Jesse's response (David's dad), "You're just a boy. Go back to tending sheep and playing the harp. This battle requires a man." Eventually Saul gives in to David's request to enter the battle. Laying aside the heavy battle armor Saul placed on him, David made a trip to the brook. I like to imagine him laying down his shepherd staff, kneeling, staring into the water, and praying, "Mighty God and Father, this battle is Yours. Give me strength for what lies ahead." Kneeling is the heart-posture of a warrior. And kneeling, he picked up five smooth stones from the stream, placed them in his shepherd's pouch, and returned to the frontlines.

David descended to the valley where the giant waited in anticipation. Goliath turned around, noticed this small pip-squeak, and began to laugh. He muttered and belched out more insults, "Is this the best you've got? I can eat this lightweight for my afternoon snack!" Intentional and direct in his anger, David took a step forward, drew a line in the sand and said, "Listen up! I come in the name of the Lord Almighty . . . the God of armies. Today, God will hand you over to me. I'll take your head off and display your dismembered body before the world. This battle is the Lord's, and the whole world will know Him today." Enraged, the giant charged the field while David readied his sling and stone. He whirled the sling, released the stone, and the giant collapsed with a mortal wound to the head (Puts new meaning to the word *stoned*). David ran over, took out Goliath's sword, and sliced off his head. The Philistines retreated, God's people advanced, and the lightweight's victory displayed God's power over evil.

Physical Battles

As a boy, did you get into any fights?

Were you ever bullied?

What did you do with your anger in those situations?

Emotional Battles

As a boy or teenager, did you experience any significant losses or disappointments with your family or friends? Disappointments with parents or siblings? Disappointments in relationships or with a girlfriend? What did you do with your anger in those situations?

Spiritual Battles

Do you remember being disappointed with God? Did you ever struggle with your faith or question your salvation?

Did you experience any losses or hurts that made you question or doubt God?

What did you do with your anger in those situations?

One of the primary emotions that marks a man's journey and the battles he faces is anger. Whether the battles are physical, emotional, or spiritual, every boy and every man faces battles in life. Hurts and disappointments typically accompany battle. And what happens? We get mad. We get angry. And what a young man does with his anger is vital to what happens in his life.

As men, there are two primary expressions of our anger: control and passivity.

Control is where a man covers his pain by spewing his anger on others. He learns that the pain of defeat or embarrassment can be covered up by pushing others away. His anger lashes out on others in potentially destructive ways. It can show up in bullying or overconfidence. It can lead a young man toward substances (alcohol or drugs) that end up controlling him. It can lead him to act out sexually (whether masturbation or sex with others or pornography). All these behaviors are rooted in anger and the desire to cover up pain or loss. Control becomes the glue for holding life together and holding yourself together.

How did your anger show up in controlling ways as a boy?

How does your anger show up in controlling ways now?

Passivity is when a man learns to bury his anger. In learning to isolate relationally, we buy into the lie that we are on our own to figure life out. This can lead to bouts with depression, even suicidal thoughts among some boys. Some live in fear of messing up or disappointing others. Some grow up in homes where explosive anger leads a young man to shut down out of fear. Others grow up in homes where peacemaking is the goal, and anger is not allowed or expressed. No matter the circumstances, every man learns to go passive with his anger. With bottled up anger, the same behaviors as noted before can show up: alcohol, drugs, sexual struggles or acting out, pornography, depression, etc. Unexpressed and unhealed anger in a man's life can become a cancer to relationship with God and others.

How did your anger show up in passive ways as a boy?

How does your anger show up in passive ways now?

Some men deal with depression (anger turned inward). If so, have you acknowledged the struggle? Have you shared that with anyone? What fears have kept you from sharing this struggle?

How do you handle anger *similar to* or *different from* the ways your dad handled or handles anger?

KNOW YOUR FRIENDSHIPS (1 SAMUEL 18—20; 2 SAMUEL 12)

Solomon, David's son, might have been reflecting on his father's life when he penned the words, "One who has unreliable friends soon comes to ruin, but there is a friend who sticks closer than a brother" (Proverbs 18:24). You can tell a lot about a man by looking at the friends who surround him. A man needs brothers, friends who will fight for him, confront him, and love him through all seasons of life. Unreliable friends bring about destruction in a man's life. Trustworthy friends protect a man's heart and life like the mighty walls around a city.

David's walk with God was bolstered by friends, two in particular, Jonathan and Nathan. Jonathan's friendship with David is illustrated in 1 Samuel 18—20. Jonathan, Saul's son, learned of the deep jealousy and hatred his father had for David. Because of David's successes, Saul developed resentment toward David and became afraid of his potential takeover. First Samuel 18 repeats the phrase, "Saul was afraid of David." Fueled by fear, Saul made several attempts to kill David. Fear of losing control or power can lead a man to take unimaginable steps and destroy innumerable lives.

As Saul's anger and jealousy built so did Jonathan's commitment to David. Defying his disloyal father, Jonathan put his own life on the line to protect David. A covenant was enacted between David and Jonathan (1 Samuel 20:16–17). And ultimately, David's life was spared because of Jonathan's brotherhood (vv. 35–42). In this telling scene of their friendship, the two of them embraced, kissed, and wept together. Jonathan then said to David, "Go in peace, for we have sworn friendship with each other in the name of the LORD" (v. 42). Now that's a friend who sticks closer than a brother.

And then there was Nathan, who functioned in a prophetic and pastoral role. Months had passed since David's sinful acts of adultery with Bathsheba and the murder of her husband Uriah. The meticulous cover up seemed to be working. That is, until God decided to confront David through his friend, Nathan. Sometimes friendship must take on tough love. In 2 Samuel 12, Nathan went to David and told a story that moved from biography to autobiography. David was confronted with his sin through the words, "You are the man" (v. 7). Nathan delivered the harsh words of judgment against David and ultimately paved the way for repentance and restoration.

Jonathan and Nathan remind us of the importance of friendship in a man's life. David needed men in his life who would support, love, confront, and protect. He needed a band of brothers to stand by his side no matter the situation.

Growing up, how would you characterize your friendships?

How would you characterize your dad's friendships?

Describe an unreliable friendship.

Describe a trustworthy friendship.

Why is it important for a man to have friends/brothers by his side?

How have you been hurt by other men in friendships?

What fears do you have about developing friendships with other men?

As a man, how would it enrich your life to have a few honest, deep friendships?

KNOW YOUR SEXUAL STORY (2 SAMUEL 11—12)

Let's begin this section with David's words from Psalm 51:16–17 (*The Message*, emphasis added): "Going through the motions doesn't please you, a flawless performance is nothing to you. I learned God-worship when my pride was shattered. *Heart-shattered lives ready for love don't for a moment escape God's notice.*" I love that last line . . . heart-shattered lives ready for love don't for a moment escape God's notice. When it comes to a man's sexual story there are layers of brokenness, shame, and hurt. Our hearts are shattered at various levels due to sexual brokenness. It is ultimately our search for love and validation that gets sexualized. We look to relationships with cravings for love, longings to be validated. And none of this escapes God's notice and God's grace.

David penned Psalm 51 on the heels of Nathan's confrontation. The story of David's life takes a major twist and turn when we come to 2 Samuel 11. Alongside the giant Goliath, there was another valley and another giant in David's life—a much more dangerous opponent in her beauty and in the subtlety in her ways. Take some time to read 2 Samuel 11 in a slow, deliberate manner. In fact, you may want to read it in several translations.

It was springtime and it was battle time. The kings were off to war and spring was in the air. The winter dull had released, flowers were blossoming, and temperatures were rising . . . in more ways than one. David, around the age of fifty, had come off a decade or so of major victories. God's kingdom was growing, and the territory was expanding. The people of Israel knew David's ways were God's ways, and His favor was resting on them. David had been a great king, a refreshing, political reprieve from the tumultuous King Saul. David had entered the battle and conquered many springtime wars. But this year, fatigue, or maybe restlessness, set in, and he decided to stay home in Jerusalem. Mistake number one.

Darkness tends to conjure up greater sexual battles for men than daylight hours. The enemy, Satan, does his best work in the dark. David, unable to sleep, decided to take a walk on the palace patio. He was restless, a bit lonely, and maybe angry inside. When a man is not in battle, his anger gets funneled in some direction. He leaned over the edge of the elevated patio, and his eyes met Bathsheba. A beauty bathing . . . and he bathed in her beauty. She was breathtaking, playful, and seemingly adventurous. His racing heart joined his thoughts, which were travelling a million directions.

Let's take a quick pause in the story. We often see Bathsheba as the innocent beauty in the story. It is possible, if not probable, that Bathsheba knew exactly what she was doing. Was she aware her bathing spot was more public than private? Was she aware King David's patio was situated just above this bathhouse? Had she peered above to see David at other times and noticed his restless heart? Her husband Uriah was out to battle. Had her heart become lonely and restless in his absence? Scripture does not answer these questions directly, but one might wonder if the affair was more two-sided than not.[10]

It is important to note that we live in a sex-saturated society. Beauty sells. Advertising agencies have latched on to this principle in their campaigns to solicit men and women's attention and pocketbooks. The money trail ultimately leads to the heart. In our longing for validation, for beauty, and for love, the world lures us into the trap of lust. The trap for a man is not sex. It is the taste of validation and the taste of adventure that draws us in. A man rarely enters the world of pornography or an affair simply looking for sex. He is looking to be loved and valued. He is looking to pursue and be pursued. The pursuit and the attached longing can lead us down some dangerous roads.

In the cool of the evening, with Bathsheba exposed below, David battles and conquers. He sends for her and sleeps with her. Adultery enters David's story. One decision. One night. One lustful pursuit . . . leads to a world of sin and trouble that wreaked havoc on David's life.

Bathsheba later discovered she was pregnant and sent word to David. Several weeks had passed, and David had tried to erase the night from his memory. Receiving the news rattled his thoughts and took him back to that night. Conviction knocked at the door, but only shame was allowed to enter. Conviction of sin, a gift from God the Father, draws us to repentance and restoration. Shame, a dagger from Satan the enemy, repels us from God and leads us to hide and bury our sin. Operating out of shame, David orchestrated a cover-up that would add murder to his résumé.

---

[10]See Swindoll, *David,* 184–185.

Uriah, Bathsheba's husband, was asked to return from battle. David hoped he would sleep with his wife during this short furlough, which will then cover all tracks and explain the pregnancy. Uriah's loyalty to David and to his country kept him on the king's doorstep. Plan A did not work. Then to plan B. David threw a lively party with all the alcohol and food a man might want. And even in a drunken stupor, Uriah's loyalty stood. He landed back on a mat outside David's door. Plan B did not work. And then David's anger drove him to a final plan of a well-designed murder scheme. With the help of Joab, David's general, and a letter instructing Uriah to be placed on the frontlines, he was killed in battle. Uriah was dead . . . murdered and removed from the thickening plot. Some weeks after the dust settled, David took Bathsheba as his wife, and all was well. David's final plan seemed to work.

And yet there is a tiny verse tucked in the end of 2 Samuel 11. Nine words that provide a haunting pause to the story: "But the thing David had done displeased the LORD" (v. 27). It was time for God to act. Instead of David doing the sending, instructing, plotting, and orchestrating, God sent Nathan.

Second Samuel 12 records the confrontation between Nathan and David and ultimately between God and David. Through the insightful use of story, or parable, Nathan invited David into a tale that became the telling of David's sin. It culminated in the declaration and verdict from Nathan's mouth, "You are the man!" (v. 7). That phrase, delivered in the courtroom of David's life, exposed the magnitude of his adultery, murder, and cover-up. Once again, conviction and shame were knocking at the door to David's heart. This time, shame was cast aside, and conviction was allowed to enter. Instead of running from the pain of his sin, David admitted and was broken. He said, "I have sinned against the LORD" (v. 13). The honesty and humility of that statement marks the life of one who lived in brokenness before God. It also foreshadows the story Jesus would tell in Luke 18 of the Pharisee and the tax collector. One prayed a self-righteous, empty prayer while the tax collector simply said, "God, have mercy on me, a sinner" (v. 13).

The prayer of brokenness in David's life would not alleviate the consequences of his sexual sin. No, God always uses consequences as a guide to fathering and loving us. Consequences are a gift from a loving Father. But that prayer did open David's heart to receive grace and restoration. It was a pivotal marker in his life.

What are your initial thoughts after walking through David's story with Bathsheba?

What are your primary emotions after reading his story of sexual sin and cover-up? (anger, fear, doubt, sadness, etc.)

Though this scene in David's life uncovers the realities of sin in a man's life, it particularly highlights the realities of sexual sin. This gives insight into David's sexual story and into every man's sexual story. The following questions guide you through your own story:

What was one of your first memories, as a boy, of something sexual?

Most boys are exposed to some level of pornography by their teenage years, whether from a department store catalog, pornographic magazine or video, or internet pornography. Were you exposed to this as a boy? How old were you? Who shared it with you? What was your response?

Were you ever sexually abused or hurt as a boy or teenager? If so, can you describe what was lost in that incident(s)? (For a man who has been sexually abused or molested, this can be a very difficult issue to write about or talk about. There is likely a lot of shame around this. You may or may not feel comfortable writing about it. It would be important to talk with a trusted friend, counselor, or pastor about this part of your story.)

How did your parents handle sexual topics and issues?

How did your dad, in particular, handle sexual topics and issues?

Did your Dad have the "sex talk" with you? If not, how did that leave you on your own? If he did, was it sufficient and healthy?

In your teenage years, describe your relationships with girls. Did you have any girlfriends? How physical or sexual were those relationships?

How have you looked to women and/or sex for a sense of value, worth, and identity?

If married, have there been sexual struggles or issues you and your wife have been unable to resolve?

As we have said before, there is a direct correlation between sexual struggles and/or hurts and a man's anger. Anger is a natural response to our losses and frustrations. How have you handled your anger over the years? (bury it, deny it, control it, etc.)

Based on David's story, what is an unhealthy response to sexual sin? Does shame draw us closer to God or push us away from God? How have you experienced shame around sexual struggles?

Based on David's story, what is a healthy response to sexual sin? Does conviction draw us closer to God or away from God? What difference would it make for you to see conviction as a loving expression from God, your Father?

KNOW YOUR GRIEF (2 SAMUEL 1; 16—18)

You can tell a lot about a man by watching the way he deals with losses and disappointments. Because of a core fear of failure, men struggle with walking honestly through our losses and our disappointments. Some of us learn to live in denial, pretending the loss wasn't that bad or didn't even exist. Some of us learn to compensate for the loss by working harder and proving our value. Because of the pain of disappointment, we often cover up our hurt and bury it deep within. In the church, many men hide or deny their losses through religious striving: becoming more disciplined, doing more Bible studies, memorizing more Scripture, serving more people, and doing more godly things. The more religious striving we do, the more a man's heart is left behind.

Grief is an important part of a man's life. How we grieve or don't grieve reveals what we do with our pain, losses, and disappointments. David's life was one filled with great victories and great heartaches. Two scenes in the David story highlight how he grieved and instruct us in our losses.

In 2 Samuel 1, David faced the loss of Saul and Saul's son, Jonathan. Even though he had turned his back on David, Saul was the former king and a former mentor. Saul wished death on David, but David still respected him. You might see Saul as a father figure in David's life who ended up inflicting many wounds. Though their relationship was never restored, David maintained a sense of respect for Saul and was able to forgive him. (This serves as a healthy example of forgiveness and grieving for those with fractured or severed relationships with their earthly fathers.)

And then there was Jonathan, Saul's son and David's closest friend. David's grief went to the deepest level when facing the loss of his soul brother and friend. It would be hard to find a closer friend and confidante in David's life. Jonathan was a man of his word, always fighting for truth in relationship. He honored his word in relationship with David and put his life on the line for his friend. When David received word about Jonathan's death, along with Saul's death, David wrote a lament and ordered the people of Judah to be taught it. You can hear David's heart in 2 Samuel 1:25–27 (emphasis added): "How the mighty have fallen in battle! Jonathan lies slain on your heights. *I grieve for you, Jonathan my brother; you were very dear to me. Your love for me was wonderful, more wonderful than that of women.* How the mighty have fallen! The weapons of war have perished!" Now that's a man who knows how to grieve. Did David bury his pain? Did he deny his losses? Did he cover up his disappointment? No, David was emotionally honest in his grief.

We also see David's grief in chapters 16 and 18 of 2 Samuel. This loss involved the death of his son, Absalom, and the accompanying pain of a fractured relationship. David and Absalom had a messy father-son relationship. Absalom eventually turned his back on his dad and sought to overtake Israel. One of the most riveting scenes takes place after Absalom's advisor Ahithophel instructed Absalom to sleep with David's concubines in the sight of all Israel (2 Samuel 16:21–22). It was a public declaration of disgust from a son to a father. It was Absalom's way of declaring what the prodigal son said in Luke 15, "Give me my share of the estate" (v. 12). *Dad, to me, you are as good as dead.*

David's response was not much better. He harbored resentment toward his son and maintained an unforgiving heart, even up to Absalom's death. Eugene Peterson describes it well:

> This is the third monumental sin of David's life, the most inexcusable, and the one for which he will pay the highest price. The adultery with Bathsheba was the affair of a passionate moment. The murder of Uriah was a royal reflex to avoid detection. But the rejection of Absalom was a steady, determined refusal to give his son what God has given David himself. Day by day he hardens in this denial of love. This is sin with a blueprint.[11]

Sin with a blueprint. A son was left wanting. And a father was left unforgiving. It was the recipe for a devastating and disastrous father-son relationship.

In 2 Samuel 18, there was a battle between David's army and Absalom's army, and Absalom eventually got caught in a large oak tree. Though David had commanded his men to be gentle with Absalom, they went against orders, took advantage of Absalom's vulnerable position, and killed him. Two servants were sent to report the news of Absalom's death to David, who immediately asked, "Is the young man Absalom safe?" (v. 29). The servants shared the news, and David was shaken. He went up to a room and wept. His words cut to the heart of grief: "O my son Absalom! My son, my son Absalom! If only I had died instead of you—O Absalom, my son, my son!" (v. 33).

What are your initial responses after reading about David's losses and his accompanying grief?

---

[11]Eugene H. Peterson, *First and Second Samuel* (Kentucky: Westminster John Knox Press, 1999), 201.

Have you dealt with the physical loss of a loved one, close friend, or family member? If so, how did you grieve or not grieve?

Have you faced any losses or disappointments in relationships? (divorce, unfaithfulness, addiction, betrayal, hurt, etc.) How did you grieve or not grieve?

What did your earthly father or mother teach you about grief? How did they handle their losses and disappointments?

If you grew up in a religious tradition or church, what were you taught about grief? How did they teach you to handle losses and disappointments?

How have you handled your grief over the years?

How might God be encouraging you to grieve past losses or current losses to move into more healing and more freedom?

Grief tends to be a mixture of sadness and anger. As David's life reminds us, every man faces heartache, loss, and disappointment. We must give ourselves room to grieve our losses. David's lament, along with several lament psalms, reminds us that grieving is an important part of the masculine journey.

KNOW YOUR ENDING (1 KINGS 1—2)

My mother Shelbie receives the newspaper each morning and turns to the obituary section first. She jokingly says, "I want to make sure my picture is not in there yet." Death is common ground for humanity. Every person is born, and every person will die. They are the bookends to life. Death plays no favorites.

I realize it sounds a bit morbid to end this chapter, "Know Self," with a section titled, "Know Your Ending." But here's the truth . . . death does not have to be a downer. If a man lives his life well and with purpose, then death is simply the exclamation mark. More than contemplating your death, it is vital for a man to contemplate his life. A life well lived in brokenness and restoration, in dependence on God's grace, is worthy of a proper ending.

We have been traveling through scenes from David's life and story. He was placed on the throne as king at thirty, he ruled for forty years, and he died at seventy. The final chapters of David's life are found in 1 Kings 1 and 2. And to be honest, his ending is messy.

Abishag, the Israeli version of hospice, was called. Abishag was a beautiful young lady brought in to function as a nurse in David's final days. She tended to his needs and brought a warm, caring presence in his last days. Absalom, the oldest son, was dead. Consequently, David's son and presumed successor, Adonijah, set himself up to succeed David as king. Like Absalom, this was no father-son relationship to place on the family mantle. It too was fractured. One of the saddest parts of David's life was the amount of family turmoil and unhealthy relationships. Certainly, David is to be celebrated as a "man after God's own heart." His walk with God should inspire all of us. But David also went to his grave surrounded by family chaos.

Adonijah created his own coronation ceremony. He was a self-made king who dishonored his father's legacy. While Absalom wanted to kill his father, Adonijah simply did not care. News of the secret coronation was shared with David on his deathbed. And at this point, Bathsheba and Nathan took charge of the situation. They approached David and reminded him of his desire and God's plan to have Solomon as the next king. This two-person cabinet advised and helped orchestrate a plan that would be best for the kingdom. Solomon was crowned as the next king.

In 1 Kings 2, we are privy to the last words from the mouth of David, which are with Solomon. They are a mixture of kindness and resentment. His initial words are filled with courage as he informs Solomon to "be strong, act like a man," and "walk in obedience to [God], and keep His decrees and commands" (vv. 2–3). He then sandwiches kindness to the sons of Barzillai between resentment toward Joab and Shimei (vv. 5–9). And then David breathed his last. He was buried with his fathers in the City of David.

The last chapter of David's life reminds us that the hero of the story is not David but God. Though David penned many incredible psalms and hymns, it was God who held the pen to his life. God writes the story. And God writes the ending. Our role? Well, we have a role to play in how we live and walk with God. David's life had some dark chapters filled with adultery, murder, lying, father wounds, and fractured family relationships. And David's life had some amazing chapters of defeating giants, walking with God, embracing brokenness, celebrating victories, living in humility, and being a great king of Israel. His life is every man's life. Your life is filled with dark chapters and celebratory chapters. God holds the pen, and He is writing the story of your life. But you have a role to play. How you live and how you handle your heart, as a man, is vital. What will be the ending to your story? What will the final chapter look like?

Reflect and journal thoughts about how you want your story to end. The phrase, "Begin with the end in mind," is a good way to approach this exercise. Then go on to answer these questions:

What kind of legacy do you want to leave behind? What do you want your wife to say about you? What do you want your children to say about you? What do you want your friends to say about you? What would you like the final chapter to look like?

Chapter 4

LIVE IN BROKENNESS AND HUMILITY

"It was a long, hot summer of racing. Your dad had driven Daisy in a handful of races. We continued to tweak the engine in hopes of getting her over the edge and into the winner's circle." Grandpa pops the hood of the old race car, props it up with a two-by-four he found in the corner, and continues the story.

"Can't tell you how many hours we spent working on this engine that summer. Before every race, we would work it over like a surgeon in the operating room. I told your dad that maybe this race would be the one."

Stepping toward Grandpa and the exposed engine, you speak up, "So Grandpa, what happened in that race? Did my dad end up winning? How did Daisy run that day?"

Staring at the engine, Grandpa says, "You know, son, it still haunts me a bit. It was the final lap of the race . . . your dad was in second, had been for a few laps. We were in the perfect spot to make a push in the final lap. In the last fuel-up, I leaned in and told your dad, 'You've got this . . . hold steady . . . and choose your timing to go for it.' With that, he sped off. Everything was in place with your dad at the wheel. Daisy had been running like never before."

Eyes wide open and smiling you chime in, "My dad was in second, going into the final lap? Wow! You must have been so excited. I can't wait to hear what happened next. How did my dad and Daisy run in the closing lap?"

Moving from the exposed engine to the other side of the car, Grandpa runs his hand slowly down the broad side of Daisy. Though you had helped push Daisy from the barn to the garage, you had never noticed this side of the race car. "You see all of these marks? She's pretty beat up over here, isn't she?"

You step around to the side and perch on your knees. "Whoa, what happened here? I didn't notice this before. She's beaten up and bruised pretty bad."

"Yep," said Grandpa, "that's what happened in the final lap. Your dad was cruising around turn four, set up to make a push to the finish line when he lost control. I don't know if it was the engine or something else, but he got loose and shaky coming out of that turn. And before I knew it, your dad collided with another car to create quite a pile-up. That was your dad and Daisy's final race."

"That was it? You mean my dad never raced again? Daisy was never repaired to make another run for it?"

Grandpa slowly kneels down on one knee, to your side. "Son, look at me; that was the race right before your dad left. Your dad was so angry and hurt. Maybe he blamed himself . . . maybe he blamed me . . . maybe he blamed Daisy. But he ran that day. Leaving town, leaving you, and leaving me. I never had the heart to put Daisy back on the track."

The garage became eerily silent, a gentle breeze glided through the front bay and traveled out the open back door.

"Grandpa, a lot of things are starting to make sense now." Both you and Grandpa rise to your feet and look at each other. "Guess this is one of the hardest parts of the story . . . Daisy's, my dad's, mine, and yours."

"You know, son," Grandpa peers deep into your eyes and soul, "men, like race cars, have to be broken down before they can be built up. Life has a way of breaking a man, humbling a man. Actually, God has a way of doing it. And as any good father knows, a son cannot become a man until he is broken. Brokenness paves the way for restoration."

"Grandpa, I never realized that working on Daisy with you was going to be so personal . . . so real. Guess I needed to learn a few things . . ."

Grandpa smirks as he pats you on the back, "Yes, all of us need to learn a few things. Well, if we don't get started on ol' Daisy, we'll never get finished. This won't be easy . . . but we need to break her down and pull everything apart. It'll be messy for a while, but eventually it will all make sense."

For when I am weak, then I am strong.

—2 Corinthians 12:10

G.I. JOE IN FLAMES!

G.I. Joe was my favorite toy and action figure growing up. I collected all the figures and accompanying tanks, guns, and military clothing I could get my hands on. I can still remember one of the camouflage tanks I spent hours playing with in the backyard. If it was camouflage, I wanted it.

These boyhood adventures did not stop with action figures and play sets. No, the boys in my neighborhood *wanted to be* G.I. Joe. We were not satisfied with the miniature world of acting; we wanted to take to the battlefield. So we did. Dressed in camo, canteen on the belt, backpack loaded with peanut butter and jelly sandwiches (our version of military MREs—Meal, Ready-to-Eat), a BB or pellet gun, and of course the infamous survival knife. Every young soldier needed a survival knife . . . just in case we got lost in the five-acre forest behind our house.

There was one particular Sunday afternoon where Matt, a neighborhood friend and son of a deacon in our church, and I decided it was time for an adventure. The woods were calling, and there was a battle to be waged. Sunday afternoon was always nap time for my parents. My dad's nap was his midafternoon break between sermons. As my parents were crawling into bed for a brief rest, I was jumping into my soldier gear preparing for battle.

Matt and I had planned our adventure that morning during children's church. Children's church stood in contrast to what we called "big church." Big church took place in the sanctuary where the congregation would sing songs and listen to a lengthy sermon. Children's church took place upstairs where we could be loud and boisterous while studying the Bible and doing crafts. I say loud and boisterous . . . actually, Mrs. Gwen rarely allowed such a thing. Mrs. Gwen was the children's church leader. She was a children's pastor before they ever invented the title. And what a saint she was. I probably learned as much about the Bible from her and the figures on the felt board as I did in seminary years later. There is a special place in heaven for servants like Mrs. Gwen.

On that Sunday, as Mrs. Gwen was teaching about Jesus calming the stormy sea and placing paper figures on the felt board, Matt and I were plotting and strategizing a battle on our internal felt boards. The plan was that we would meet at my house directly after Sunday lunch. I would bring the peanut butter and jelly sandwiches, and he'd bring the matches. Oh, did I mention soldiers carry matches?

Lunch was over, and my parents were retiring to their bedroom quarters for their midday nap. With all my gear on, guns "loaded," and canteen filled, I was an eight-year old G.I. Joe. And I felt like it. I felt powerful and dangerous. Off to the kitchen to make the sandwiches, slide them in a plastic bag, and load them in the army backpack. We were now ready for battle.

Matt showed up, and we were quickly off to the back woods. My family lived in Thomaston, Georgia, at the time, in the church parsonage. Behind the house was a small forest where we would often play war. On this day, Matt and I entered the forest, armed and dangerous. We climbed trees, shot stuff, hid in bunkers, and annihilated the enemy. These woods were a boy's paradise. And after the battle was over, we retired under a large shade tree . . . our version of the mess hall. I went to pull out the peanut butter and jelly sandwiches when suddenly I was struck with an idea. *I wonder what these sandwiches would taste like if toasted?* After all that we had been through on the battlefield, we deserved the best. No soldier should settle for a meager PB&J. We needed the toasted upgrade. And that's where the matches came in to play.

We made a fire for the great toast to a great day of war. Now, I failed to mention earlier that I was a Cub Scout. There was only one problem. I was absent the week they talked about building a campfire and the need to avoid placing your fire pit under the shade of a large, dry, leafy, oak tree. We built what we thought was a relatively small fire. Building a fire, though, after a long, hot, and dry summer can be a bit testy. Before we knew it, the fire was spreading and growing. We pulled out our canteens and quickly emptied them on the flames. Then we went to grabbing handfuls of dirt to try and squelch the fire. It looked like we were tossing gasoline on the fire instead of water and dirt. The flames continued to spread.

At some point in our soldier-turned-firefighter experience, I realized we needed some help. I ran to our house and rushed into my parents' bedroom. With the aroma of smoke arriving just before me, my blackened hands and soot-smothered face awakened my parents from a nice nap. The words rushed out of my mouth, "The woods are on fire! The woods are on fire!" My dad jumped out of bed and looked out the window. My declaration was confirmed.

The fire department was called, and it seemed as though every church member within a fifty-mile range arrived at our house. Eventually the fire was put out and everyone returned to their homes. With head hanging low, I began the long walk toward our house where I knew a "rear-end alignment" was awaiting me.

I honestly cannot remember what the church service was like that night at our little Baptist church. I don't know if my dad pulled out a sermon on hell to highlight the flames of his Sunday afternoon. I can't remember if Matt and I walked the aisle, rededicating our lives to God while committing to go on the mission field. I just remember that Sunday as the Sunday afternoon G.I. Joe went up in flames.

All of us have stories from childhood where we reenacted the life of some superhero. What were your childhood heroes? Batman and Robin, Superman, the Lone Ranger, Spider-Man, Luke Skywalker, Iron Man, The Incredible Hulk, or G.I. Joe? There is something wired into the fabric of a man that makes us want to be powerful. We want to come through and be a part of some great adventure.

God has blessed me with three sons: Caleb, Brennan, and Asher. Though each has a unique personality, they all share the common goal of wanting to be great, to be powerful. Caleb wants to be a star basketball player and get a book published. Brennan loves anything camouflage and is an aspiring entrepreneur. If there's a way to make a dollar, he will figure it out. Asher is into Spider-Man and currently wants to crash anything he can get his hands on. Watching them reminds me of my own childhood and of the desires God has planted in a man's heart. Every man wants to be powerful.

Whether you have a son or have witnessed young boys playing, how have you seen the desire to be powerful? Give a few examples.

UPSIDE-DOWN THEOLOGY

There are many truths in the Bible that seem upside down. Jesus talked about the first being last and last being first, the least being the greatest, and the ordinary doing extraordinary things. One of the greatest upside-down truths of Christianity is that weakness brings strength, and brokenness paves the way for power. Scripture is filled with examples of God using the disqualified, the misfit, and the outcast. *The weak are containers for the power of God.* In the kingdom of God, "the one thing that qualifies you is knowing you are weak, and the one thing that disqualifies you is thinking you are strong."[12] Listen to this biblical truth:

> Time and again the biblical storyline is one not of God being frustrated by human weakness but attracted to it. This encompasses not only natural weakness (birthplace, tribal association, speech deficiency, natural timidity) but also moral weakness (deceit, adultery, murder, prostitution, fear). The point is not that God lowers what we perceive to be the standard by which his favor is attained but that, because of Christ, he inverts that standard.[13]

It is not a matter of qualifying ourselves; instead, God's power is made known through the disqualified in Scripture. Whatever the weakness may be, God's power is fully experienced through our brokenness and weakness.

This biblical truth runs against the grain of what culture tells a man to do to be powerful. Success, fame, promotions, titles, wealth, and prestige are methods used to prop ourselves up. This flimsy scaffolding will eventually fall. It simply does not work and will not last. What God offers a man is the opportunity to experience life, strength, and power through the avenue of brokenness and humility. *The third phase of restoration in a man's journey is to live in brokenness and humility, which leads to experiencing God's power.* If a man wants to be powerful, he must live in brokenness and humility.

When you first hear, "live in brokenness," what comes to mind?

---

[12]Dane Ortlund, "Power Is Made Perfect in Weakness: A Biblical Theology of Strength through Weakness," *Presbyterion* 36/2 (Fall 2010): 98.
[13]Ortlund, 107.

How does this stand in contrast to what the world says makes a man powerful?

Let's begin with a birds-eye view of this theme in Scripture. Those considered less than, overlooked, or ill-equipped become containers for grace and power. At the heart of this biblical theme of brokenness is God's desire to show "mercy to those whom society least expects to receive it and uses the weak to confute the strong."[14] God's choosing of the "weak" or "younger" shows how God's power is experienced. One author sheds light on this biblical theme:

> The election of the younger is God's inscrutable device of choosing whom He will, the last-born in place of the first. This is his built-in correction of the possible abuse growing out of the law which is meant to establish justice and sometime does not. The folk love such stories because they are a weapon against the powerful, complacent and learned authorities. God, the stories tell us, chose the patriarchs as He pleased, i.e, the folk who created these stories said that God passed over the oldest and chose the youngest.[15]

Moses, Gideon, David, and Solomon—none of these biblical giants were firstborn sons.[16] This is not to be taken as a literal favoring of the lastborn over the firstborn. In this culture, the firstborn received all the familial privileges while the youngest was often overlooked.

---

[14]Frank Thielman, "Unexpected Mercy: Echoes of a Biblical Motif in Romans 9—11," *Scottish Journal of Theology* 47, no. 2 (May 1994): 181.

[15]Judah Goldin, "The Youngest Son or Where Does Genesis 38 Belong," *Journal of Biblical Literature* 96 no. 1 (1977): 44.

[16]Goldin, 34.

God turned this manmade system upside down by showing power through those who society considered weak.

In the Pentateuch (first five books of the Old Testament), God often chose the weak to lead His people and demonstrate His power. Abraham, who considered himself "dust and ashes" (Genesis 18:27), was chosen to be the father of many nations. In fact, the Abrahamic covenant (Genesis 17) is rooted in God's seed of faith flourishing through a ninety-nine-year-old man.[17] Moses, the younger, adopted brother who was raised in Pharaoh's palace, was elevated to political status and then humbled through murderous actions. After forty years of shepherding in "no-man's land," Moses received a call from God to lead His people, and he responded with, "Who am I that I should go to Pharaoh?" (Exodus 3:11). Humility is fertile soil for strength. Later, the Mosaic covenant, or Ten Commandments (Exodus 20), is provided as a necessary boundary for incredibly weak people. God's law and its power are enacted among the sinful, weak nation of Israel. *The first books of the Old Testament declare power through weakness.*

And this theme continues. In Judges 6:15, Gideon's family was the "weakest in Manasseh," and he was the "least" in his family. Yet God's power was demonstrated through Gideon's defeat of the Midianites. David, the youngest and most overlooked of Jesse's sons, was chosen to be Israel's king (1 Samuel 16). In response to Saul's potential promotion of David after defeating Goliath, David said, "I'm only a poor man and little known" (1 Samuel 18:23). David's natural

---

[17]Thielman, "Unexpected Mercy," 176–177. Thielman notes: "The surprise then comes with God's announcement to Abraham that although Ishmael would become a great people, God would keep his promise to Abraham not through the first born but through the second born son." The same "echoes" are heard related to the birth of Jacob and Esau. "God chooses to fulfill his promise through the second born, Jacob, rather than through the first born, Esau."

weakness was a container for God's power. His power is equally demonstrated through David's moral weakness. With adultery and murder on his résumé, David shepherded God's people and became a vital link in Jesus' lineage. The Davidic covenant (2 Samuel 7) built the foundation for God to plant His power and mercy in the heart of a weak, sinful man and nation.

The Psalms and the Prophets declare the power of God manifested through weakness. God is close to the "brokenhearted" (Psalm 34:18) and is with those who walk through the "darkest valley" (23:4). In Psalm 51, David declared the mercy and unfailing love of God amid his sin-saturated life. The prophet Isaiah declared God dwells with the "contrite and lowly in spirit" (Isaiah 57:15) and looks to the "humble and contrite in spirit" (66:2). The suffering servant of Isaiah 61 comes to "proclaim good news to the poor," "bind up the brokenhearted," "proclaim freedom for the captives," "release from darkness for the prisoners," and "comfort all who mourn" (vv. 1–2). The prophet Hosea's life and marriage were living images of God's power to restore what is broken. These poetic and prophetic voices herald the message of God's power demonstrated through the lowly, broken, and weak. *Are you starting to see the pattern of God showing power through the broken and humble?*

Arriving at the New Testament, this theme of power in weakness is seen immediately in the genealogy of Christ. Women are included, most of whom had a troubled story and past. There was Tamar (Genesis 38), Rahab (Joshua 2 and 6), Ruth, and Bathsheba (2 Samuel 11—12). Luke scripts his Gospel in such a way to highlight the role of the social outcasts in Jesus' ministry: tax collectors, prostitutes, women, Gentiles, etc. Luke then builds on the Old Testament theme of God choosing the weak or younger alluded to earlier when the father welcomes the younger son home while the older brother remains alienated (Luke 15).

The Apostle John provides, more than the other Gospels, a lengthy treatment of Jesus' journey to the Cross—itself a demonstration of power through weakness. The Cross, a symbol of offense and weakness, is the place of strength and power through the sacrificial death of Jesus Christ. It is through the apparent weakness of Christ that the power of salvation is made available. Our response of faith "entails a candid admission of weakness—that peace with God comes not through one's own efforts to propitiate [satisfy] his wrath or to earn some payment from him but through embracing the initiative that God has taken in his Son Jesus Christ to restore his fallen creatures to himself."[18] The Gospel writers speak with one unifying voice, "That it was through his weakness that Christ was ultimately glorified. His shame was ultimately the means, not an obstacle, to his honor."[19]

The remaining sections of the New Testament continue and build on this theme of power through weakness. Paul's message is that "God chose the foolish things of the world to shame the wise; God chose the weak things of the world to shame the strong" (1 Corinthians 1:27). Many of Paul's letters were written to those who were weak in the sufferings of Christ. The New Testament writings culminate in the Book of Revelation with the recurring image of the Lamb, a seemingly weak animal, who puts a final exclamation to God's power.

Whew . . . I know that was a lot to take in. But I want you to see how this theme of "power through the broken and humble" runs

---

[18]Frank Thielman, *Theology of the New Testament: A Canonical and Synthetic Approach* (Grand Rapids: Zondervan, 2005), 698.
[19]Ortlund, "Power is Made Perfect in Weakness," 103.

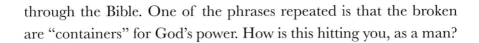

through the Bible. One of the phrases repeated is that the broken are "containers" for God's power. How is this hitting you, as a man?

Does this biblical theme of living in brokenness and humility unsettle you, make you nervous, or incite fear?

In your own words, summarize the biblical theme of power through brokenness.

Men want to be powerful. That is a desire placed there by God. A man wants to come through, compete, and overcome. The examples from Scripture remind us that a man must come to the end of himself and realize his own brokenness and weakness. This recognition of weakness paves the way for the power of God. Humility brings power.

How do you fight against revealing weakness?

What frightens you about revealing weakness to God, other men, or your spouse?

Pride repels; brokenness attracts. Our brokenness is what unites us as men and paves the way for God's power. How honest have you been with your community of men or with another man? Why are you afraid of admitting brokenness to others?

STEP 1: ADMIT BROKENNESS AND CHOOSE HUMILITY

A psalm of David. When the prophet Nathan came to him after David had committed adultery with Bathsheba.

> Have mercy on me, O God,
>   according to your unfailing love;
> according to your great compassion
>   blot out my transgressions.
> Wash away all my iniquity
>   and cleanse me from my sin.
> For I know my transgressions,
>   and my sin is always before me.
> Against you, you only, have I sinned
>   and done what is evil in your sight;

so you are right in your verdict
    and justified when you judge.
Surely I was sinful at birth,
    sinful from the time my mother conceived me.
Yet you desired faithfulness even in the womb;
    you taught me wisdom in that secret place.
Cleanse me with hyssop, and I will be clean;
    wash me, and I will be whiter than snow.
Let me hear joy and gladness;
    let the bones you have crushed rejoice.
Hide your face from my sins
    and blot out all my iniquity.
Create in me a pure heart, O God,
    and renew a steadfast spirit within me.
Do not cast me from your presence
    or take your Holy Spirit from me.
Restore to me the joy of your salvation
    and grant me a willing spirit, to sustain me.
Then I will teach transgressors your ways,
    so that sinners will turn back to you.
Deliver me from the guilt of bloodshed, O God,
    you who are God my Savior,
    and my tongue will sing of your righteousness.
Open my lips, Lord,
    and my mouth will declare your praise.
You do not delight in sacrifice, or I would bring it;
    you do not take pleasure in burnt offerings.
My sacrifice, O God, is a broken spirit;
    a broken and contrite heart
    you, God, will not despise.
May it please you to prosper Zion,
    to build up the walls of Jerusalem.

Then you will delight in the sacrifices of the righteous,
in burnt offerings offered whole;
then bulls will be offered on your altar.

—Psalm 51

How do we become powerful through brokenness and humility? To break it down, we are going to look at three steps: (1) admit brokenness and choose humility based on Psalm 51; (2) embrace God's process for restoration based on Hosea 2; and (3) receive power in weakness based on 2 Corinthians 12.

David wrote Psalm 51 during one of the darkest hours of his life—on the heels of adultery with Bathsheba and the murder of her husband Uriah (2 Samuel 11—12). In it, David models how he admitted his own brokenness and chose humility by *confession*, *restoration*, and *leadership*. *Confession*, the admission of weakness and moral failure, fills the initial verses. He owns his mistakes instead of denying them. He declares his transgressions, iniquity, and sin. In doing so, David is not referring to an event but to the condition of his heart. He says he was "sinful at birth, sinful from the time [his] mother conceived [him]" (v. 5). To live in brokenness and humility, a man must be willing to own his mistakes and sin. Think of sin as not merely the things you do but the condition of your masculine heart.

I often use the phrase, "We're all jacked up!" I guess that's my way of admitting brokenness. The world leads a man to cover up weakness by compensating with success or fame. I don't know about you, but I am more trusting of men who admit their weaknesses versus men who try to sell me on their successes. And this covering up of weakness also takes place in the church. When men gather, our tendency is to give the cordial, "Doing fine!" David reminds us in this psalm to be men who own their stuff and admit we're "jacked up" too. I love verse 17 where David declares that God is looking for broken spirits and broken hearts. Pride repels God while brokenness invites God.

Confession brings *restoration*. I'm so glad the psalm moves to restoration and healing. There is hope for broken men. In verse 10, the transition happens. David pleaded with God to "create in [him] a pure heart" and then to "restore to [him] the joy of your salvation" (v. 12). *Create (bara* in Hebrew) is only used of God and is reminiscent of Genesis 1. God is being asked to do what only He can do: create something out of nothing. And God always answers the honest prayer from a broken man's heart.

This is where the process of restoration and healing takes place. We will talk about that process in the next step. For now, we focus on the asking. In admitting our brokenness and sin, we are also asking God to heal our hearts. How are you at asking for help? I'm guessing you're like me . . . it is hard to ask for help. Pride says to do it on my own. Self-reliance says, "I've got this!" But living in brokenness and humility leads me to ask for help. I am asking God to do what I cannot do on my own. He is the source of healing and power. He is the source of grace. Prayer is not merely asking God for stuff but asking God to father me, heal me, and restore me.

Restoration brings *leadership*. Because of God's power, David says he will "teach transgressors [God's] ways, so that sinners will to turn back to you" (v. 13). The natural flow from confession to restoration leads a man to offer this power and hope to others. As a man admits brokenness and chooses humility, he is then able to help others experience God's power. Confession . . . restoration . . . leadership.

There is a greater purpose to your story and to your restoration. God is not rebuilding you just for you. God did not heal my marriage just for me. I remember the day so clearly. It was a few years removed from the affairs. Melody and I both heard God say, "I want to use your broken story and broken lives to bring healing to others." To be honest, we both started laughing when we shared what each of us was hearing. God wants to use us? He wants us to share our messed-up story with others? Good can come out of our bad? We stepped out in faith and began to share our story and fight for others who were hurting. Even as I write today, I am still amazed that God does His work through broken people like us. He has, He can, and He will use broken, humble people to do His work.

What stood out as you walked through Psalm 51?

Knowing David's story and the tragic scene with Bathsheba, what emotion do you hear in this psalm?

What does this psalm teach you about brokenness and God's power?

Confession: In your own words, what does it mean for a man to confess and be open about his sin, struggles, and weaknesses?

Restoration: God fathers and restores broken men. How would you describe a man who is being restored?

Leadership: David goes on to say, "Restore to me the joy of your salvation . . . Then I will teach transgressors your ways" (vv. 12–13). The purpose of your healing is not just for you but also for others. God's power flowed through David to others. How has God used another person to encourage you? How might God use your life and story to encourage another person?

I am sure David would have preferred to edit or delete the Bathsheba scene from his story—sexual sin, murder, loss. What scenes in your story would you like to edit or delete?

Listen closely. The scenes in your story you most want to delete may contain the vital elements to your healing and freedom. Instead of overlooking, editing, or deleting, God wants access to your brokenness and to your masculine heart. Will you choose to be honest with God and let Him father you?

STEP 2: EMBRACE GOD'S PROCESS FOR RESTORATION

"Rebuke your mother, rebuke her, for she is not my wife, and I am not her husband. Let her remove the adulterous look from her face and the unfaithfulness from between her breasts. Otherwise I will strip her naked and make her as bare as on the day she was born; I will make her like a desert, turn her into a parched land, and slay her with thirst. I will not show my love to her children, because they are the children of adultery. Their mother has been unfaithful and has conceived them in disgrace. She said, 'I will go after my lovers, who give me my food and my water, my wool and my linen, my olive oil and my drink.' Therefore I will block her path with thornbushes; I will wall her in so that she cannot find her way. She will chase after her lovers but not catch them; she will look for them but not find them. Then she will say, 'I will go back to my husband as at first, for then I was better off than now.' She has not acknowledged that I was the one who gave her the grain, the new wine and oil, who lavished on her the silver and gold—which they used for Baal. Therefore I will take away my grain when it ripens, and my new wine when it is ready. I will take back my wool and my linen, intended to cover her naked body. So now I will expose her lewdness before the eyes of her lovers; no one will take her out of my hands. I will stop all her celebrations: her yearly festivals, her New Moons, her Sabbath days—all her appointed festivals. I will ruin her vines and her fig trees, which she said were her pay from her lovers; I will make them a thicket, and wild animals will devour them. I will punish her for the days she burned incense to the Baals; she decked herself with rings and jewelry, and went after her lovers, but me she forgot," declares the LORD. "*Therefore I am now going to allure her; I will lead her into the wilderness and speak tenderly to her. There I will give her back her vineyards, and will make the Valley of Achor [trouble] a door of hope. There she will respond as in the days of her youth, as in the day she came up out of Egypt.* In that day," declares the LORD, "you will call me 'my husband'; you will no longer call me 'my master.' I will remove the names of the Baals from her lips; no longer will their names be invoked. In that day I will make a covenant for them with the beasts of the field, the birds in the sky and the creatures that move along the ground. Bow and sword and battle I will abolish from the land, so that all may lie down in safety. I will betroth you to me forever; I will betroth you in righteousness and justice, in love and compassion. I will betroth you in faithfulness, and you will acknowledge the LORD. In that day I will respond," declares the LORD—"I will respond to the skies, and they will respond to the earth; and the earth will respond to the grain, the new wine and the olive oil, and they will respond to Jezreel. I will plant her for myself in the land; I will show my love to the one I called 'Not my loved one.' I will say to those called 'Not my people,' 'You are my people'; and they will say, 'You are my God.'"

—Hosea 2:2–23 (emphasis added)

It may have been the most difficult moment of my life. The night before, our marriage had collapsed. Melody's affair was exposed and my passivity and weaknesses surfaced. We were only hours removed from the tragedy. After spending a sleepless night at a friend's house, I decided to look at the one-year Bible I had been reading for a few years. Turning to that day's entry, I was emotionally numb and lifeless. Facing the loss of my marriage and the collapse of my masculine heart, I wondered if God was even there. Did He care? Had he forgotten me?

The day's reading was the story of Hosea. I was mildly familiar with this story about a man called to pursue his wife and marriage. A story of loss. A story of restoration. And I was angry. I tossed the Bible across the room and said, "God, don't do this. I'm done." To be honest, I don't even know why I opened the Bible that day. I wasn't really looking to hear from God, but He spoke anyway. What did I hear God say? *Stay in the game . . . keep pursuing . . . don't give up on your marriage . . . don't give up on Me.* It was both the worst and best day of my life. My life and marriage felt like a complete lie, but God did what I could not do. He gave me hope in the midst of total loss. He gave me strength when I was without an ounce of emotional energy. And He gave me a process.

I ended up spending a lot of time in Hosea over the coming weeks. I wrestled with God a lot. Felt a bit like Jacob in Genesis 32 when he wrestled with an angel and would not let go. I wasn't going to let go until God showed me a greater purpose for my pain. At first, the Hosea story put me in the role of Hosea . . . a man fighting for his marriage. I was being asked to pursue, love, and forgive. Not overnight. But through a process, God fathered me in how to truly love my wife and forgive her.

And then the Hosea story put me in the role of Gomer, the unfaithful wife. It did not take long before I realized my place in the story was no different from Melody's place in the story. God was and is the Hosea figure, the forgiving one. He authors the story and is the hero of the story. I am the broken one. I am the one who has been unfaithful, unrelenting in my sinful pursuits, and hardened of heart. I was and am Gomer . . . desperate and in need of restoration. Our marriage being restored was going to take more than Melody dealing with her stuff. God took me on a journey of dealing with me. It was a process of going back to go forward . . . unearthing my story and past to receive healing and restoration. You heard a lot of that in the first few chapters.

In order to complete step two and embrace God's process for restoration, we must focus on a key word: *process.* In the introduction, we talked about points versus process. We also said God wants to father you more than fix you. Hosea 2 is a great place for us to spend some time understanding God's way of growing us. Aren't you glad God is in the business of rebuilding broken men? Like me . . . like you.

Hosea joins the biblical symphony of power in weakness. Among the prophets, Hosea's message was unique because his marriage was meant to mirror God's relationship with His people. Hosea, whose name means help or deliverance,[20] is called by God to take an adulterous wife (Gomer) (Hosea 1). Gomer's lifestyle was a metaphor for the filthy, sinful hearts of the Israelites. Hosea 1 reminds us that sin is more than missing the mark or making a few mistakes. Sin, like adulterous Gomer, is a condition of the human heart. Remember our phrase, "We're all jacked up."

We now arrive at Hosea 2. Similar to Psalm 51, Hosea 2 unfolds in two parts: exposure of sin and restoration.[21] The first thirteen verses present God as the husband who has been betrayed. I have to be honest . . . these are hard verses to read. God is exposing Gomer in her adulterous actions. From revealing her false lovers to surrounding her with thornbushes, God allows consequences to lay heavy on her.

The exposure of sin is one of the more challenging parts of God's process of restoring a man's heart. Brokenness comes through waves of conviction and consequences in our lives. God will, at times, *allow* consequences and, at other times, *orchestrate* consequences. We must keep in focus that God is our loving Father. Without that understanding, God can feel harsh and distant. But remember the section from David's life on anger? Anger is connected to love. The most loving person will be angry when betrayed.

God's process does involve exposing our sin, false lovers, and even our empty religious acts. To live in brokenness and humility, we must have a healthy framework for the process of growth. Brokenness

---

[20]Theo. Laetsch, *The Minor Prophets* (Saint Louis: Concordia Publishing House, 1956), 9.

[21]See Walter Brueggemann, "The Recovering God of Hosea," *Horizons in Biblical Theology* 30, no. 1 (2008): 15, 18.

paves the way for restoration. Humility comes in a man's life when he is faced with the depth of his own broken heart and empty religious efforts. Sin in our lives must be exposed to deal with pride. Empty religious efforts must be thwarted so God can get beyond behavioral changes and heal a man's heart.

If Hosea 2 ended at verse 13, we would be left with an angry, unresolved relationship. We would be left with a jaded, distorted image of God. Gomer, a picture of Israel, has been completely exposed in her unfaithfulness and moral weakness. The punishment of abandonment would certainly fit the crime.[22] Instead, we find one of the most amazing pictures of grace in verses 14 and 15: "Therefore I am now going to allure [seduce, romance, entice] her; I will lead her into the wilderness and speak tenderly to her. There I will give her back her vineyards, and will make the Valley of Achor [trouble] a door of hope. There she will respond as in the days of her youth, as in the day she came up out of Egypt." Reminiscent of the Great Exodus, God would deliver His people from their destructive destiny.[23] Instead of cutting off the relationship, God uses the process to rebuild and restore.

God's process for rebuilding a man involves exposing our sinful, prideful ways. This creates brokenness and humility. Once there, He joyfully delivers power to the weak and grace to the humble. Remember our phrase, only the broken/humble are proper containers for the grace of God. Emptied of self . . . filled with God's power.

We began this chapter talking about the desire within every man to be powerful. I think we can all agree with that. Whether in sports,

---

[22]Douglas Stuart, *Word Biblical Commentary: Hosea–Jonah* (Waco: Word Books, 1987), 48. "The normal punishment for adultery in ancient Israel was either burning (Gen 38:24; Lev 21:9) or stoning (Deut 22:23–24)."

[23]Derek Kidner, *The Message of Hosea: Love to the Loveless* (Downers Grove: InterVarsity Press, 1981), 32.

our jobs, or hobbies, we have a desire to come through and win. It is wired into masculinity. Hosea 2 gives us a process whereby a man can become powerful in God's strength and in God's grace.

What is your first reaction to studying Hosea 2?

The first half of Hosea 2 (verses 2–13) involves God exposing Gomer in her sin and adultery. This is God's way of exposing our false lovers and drawing us to Himself. How would you explain that exposure as an act of love?

There is a great difference between conviction and guilt. Guilt comes from the enemy, Satan, and spirals a man into greater sin. Guilt brings condemnation. God, conversely, fathers through conviction and discipline. This is what a good father does. How has God convicted or disciplined you? How is He currently convicting or disciplining you?

Have you viewed conviction through the lens of a loving father?

God's desire is to turn the wilderness into a vineyard. He desires to make the valley of trouble into a doorway of hope. As a man, what wilderness are you struggling through right now? What anger do you have about this wilderness? Will you choose to trust that God is fathering and doing a good work of restoration in your masculine heart?

STEP 3: RECEIVE POWER IN WEAKNESS

> Therefore, in order to keep me from becoming conceited, I was given a thorn in my flesh, a messenger of Satan, to torment me. Three times I pleaded with the Lord to take it away from me. But he said to me, "My grace is sufficient for you, for my power is made perfect in weakness." Therefore I will boast all the more gladly about my weaknesses, so that Christ's power may rest on me. That is why, for Christ's sake, I delight in weaknesses, in insults, in hardships, in persecutions, in difficulties. For when I am weak, then I am strong.
>
> —2 Corinthians 12:7–10

For a long time, I have carried a metal stake in my vehicle. Being a visual person, I need tangible reminders of what it means to be a man, God's kind of man. It's the kind of stake used to secure railroad ties. You've probably seen these lying beside a railroad track, rusty and brown from the weather. Why would I carry something like this? It keeps me planted firm in the Restored Man truth from

2 Corinthians 12: God gives power to the weak. Let's look at this powerful passage from our brother Paul.

The New Testament includes two of Paul's letters to the church at Corinth. In the second letter, Paul dealt with some specific issues the church was facing. At this particular time and place, boasting was a way to promote self. Whether through highlighting health, wealth, or prominence, this first-century culture loved to glorify self. And "In Corinth, perhaps more than anywhere else, social ascent was the goal, boasting and self-display the means, personal power and glory the reward."[24]

I think you are starting to see that Corinth was a first-century version of America. Whether through our jobs, social media, money, or sports, a man is drawn to glory in himself. We like to prop ourselves up through social status, sing our praises through a resounding résumé, and fill the posts of a social media outlet with our accomplishments and fantasy lives. We American men like ourselves . . . a lot. And so did the Corinthians.

Like the surrounding culture, the church in Corinth wanted Paul to declare his merits. They wanted him to boast in the many revelations he had received. This would give them authority and power over others.

In contrast to reveling in strengths or posting a nice religious résumé, Paul chose to boast in his weaknesses. The particular weakness Paul referred to in 2 Corinthians 12 is a "thorn [*skolops*][25]

---

[24]Timothy B. Savage, *Power Through Weakness: Paul's Understanding of the Christian Ministry in 2 Corinthians* (Cambridge: Cambridge University Press, 1996), 41.

[25]*Skolop* may be translated "thorn" or more accurately "stake." See David M. Park, "Thorn or Stake?" *Novum Testamentum*, Vol. 22, fasc. 2 (April 1980): 179–183. See also Alexandra R. Brown, "The Gospel Takes Place: Paul's Theology of Power-in-Weakness in 2 Corinthians," *Interpretation, Vol.* 52 (July 1998): 271–285 as the author treats the "place" of Paul's power in affliction.

in the flesh," which is used by God to "pin" him to Christ.[26] Like me, you are probably wondering what this thorn was in Paul's life. Some have viewed it as a physical struggle such as a pain in the ear or head, or even epilepsy. Many think it refers to Paul's opponents[27] or some say a spiritual temptation. Others have seen it as an ongoing sexual temptation since Paul was a single man.

While we do not know the exact nature of this thorn/stake, we do know it was both inherently evil and a gift from God. It was a struggle . . . a part of Paul's story he wanted to edit out. He asked God three times to remove it. Instead, God was able to use this struggle to deliver His power. God says to Paul, "My grace is sufficient for you, for my power is made perfect in weakness" (v. 9). Did we catch that? God's power is made perfect . . . His strength gets delivered . . . in weakness.

I want to look closely at one word in verse 9. Paul says God's power *rests* on him. The word *rests* literally means to "tabernacle" or "hover over" something or someone. In the Old Testament, when God's people journeyed through the wilderness or desert, they set up temporary places of worship called tabernacles. God's presence traveled with them and literally hovered over the tabernacle. Paul is saying God's power hovers over, rests on, those who live in brokenness and humility.

OK, so what is the relationship between thorns/stakes, weakness, and God's power? What's the significance of my metal stake? Just like Paul, you and I have things in our lives that usher in brokenness. Some of our brokenness comes from our own mistakes and failures. We have all messed up in various ways, hurting ourselves and others, while other parts of our brokenness as men comes from the mistakes and failures of others. Whether hurts from our childhood or teen

---

[26]Barnett, *The Message of 2 Corinthians*, 176–180.

[27]An example would be the Judaizers, a religious group, wreaking havoc on Paul's ministry in Galatia.

years or heartaches in adulthood, each of us has been hurt by the sins of others.

Second Corinthians 12 declares a truth about men and brokenness. Instead of hiding your brokenness and hurts or compensating through work, relationships, or religion, God's power is given to the weak, the broken, the humble. To live in brokenness is to be defined by God more than by our mistakes. To live in humility is to look to God's grace more than human efforts for restoration.

If you and I want to be power-full men . . . if we want to have God's strength flowing through us . . . then we must live in brokenness and humility.

What does 2 Corinthians 12 teach you about God's power through brokenness?

Why was Paul given a thorn/stake in the flesh? Why would God allow something like that to happen? How might God's allowing of hardship or hurts distort a person's view of God?

What about you? What would you characterize as a thorn in your life? Is there something that continually troubles you, something you wish you could delete from your life? It could be a past memory or mistake. It could be a relationship. It could be something internal that causes tension, anxiety, or fear. What are some of your thorns?

How might God want to demonstrate His power through your thorn, your weakness?

Paul actually boasted in his thorn and his weaknesses. His résumé was not built on human accomplishments or accolades. It was built on brokenness. What do you tend to boast in?

As a man, what is God saying about living in brokenness as it relates to experiencing His power?

How would living in brokenness and humility affect your relationship with God?

If married, how would your marriage look different if you lived in brokenness and humility?

How might others benefit from your weakness, instead of your "having it together"?

Chapter 5

WALK WITH GOD IN THE DISCIPLINES

"Grandpa, this color looks really nice. Daisy is starting to look like her old self again. Or maybe I should say . . . 'new self.'"

"You know, son, we've been working on Daisy for several months now. Engine seems to be running smooth. New set of tires. And that broken side . . . Well, it looks pretty nice, doesn't it?"

"Sure does. To be honest, I wondered if we could ever get this damaged side to look good again. She sure was banged up from that wreck. But we did it, Grandpa. Wow, we did it."

Grandpa chimes in, "Do you remember, months ago, when you were down in the barn . . . right after you found Daisy?"

"Definitely. I never even knew you had a race car. Or that my dad was a race car driver. I'll never forget that day."

Gently smiling your way, Grandpa says, "And remember we sat down on those buckets and talked about doing this whole restoration project together. Before pushing her up to the garage, I asked you the reason for doing this . . ."

"I do remember that. I was confused at first. Guess I thought the purpose of this was to restore ol' Daisy." Pausing for a moment, your mind revisits the hours and days spent in this garage with your grandfather. "You know, I've learned a lot over these months. Your story . . . my dad's story. Learned a lot about myself. I guess the point was never about the restoration but about our relationship, wasn't it?"

Grandpa throws that long arm around you, "Ah, son, you've got that right. The time with you has been so good for me. I wasn't always the best father to your dad. Made some mistakes along the way. This old garage reminds me of my own scars, hurts, and failures. But now I have some new memories . . . memories with you."

"Guess we're both a lot more like Daisy than we realized." Walking over to the race car and placing your right hand on the steering wheel, you consider the similarities. "Been through some hard times . . . beat up and damaged. Wrecked and stored in an old barn. But now . . . look at Daisy . . . look at us." Looking over at Grandpa you say, "I have to admit . . . being restored is a messy and long process. But it's worth it. Definitely worth it."

Slowly moving over to Daisy and placing his left hand on the hood and running his right hand over your head, Grandpa says, "I'm so proud of you, son." Pulling you close with a gentle hug, he adds, "Hope I've been a bit of a father to you. This old garage has become like a sanctuary for us. Time and space for us to build a relationship . . . guess you could say a father-son relationship. You're right, it's definitely been worth it."

"Well," Grandpa says, "Daisy needs some final touches. Let's get to work and finish things up."

In this all-out match against sin, others have suffered far worse than you, to say nothing of what Jesus went through—all that bloodshed! So don't feel sorry for yourselves. Or have you forgotten how good parents treat children, and that God regards you as *his* children? My dear child, don't shrug off God's discipline, but don't be crushed by it either. It's the child he loves that he disciplines; the child he embraces, he also corrects. God is educating you; that's why you must never drop out. He's treating you as dear children. This trouble you're in isn't punishment; it's *training*, the normal experience of children. Only irresponsible parents leave children to fend for themselves. Would you prefer an irresponsible God? We respect our own parents for training and not spoiling us, so why not embrace God's training so we can truly *live*? While we were children, our parents did what *seemed* best to them. But God is doing what *is* best for us, training us to live God's holy best. At the time, discipline isn't much fun. It always feels like it's going against the grain. Later, of course, it pays off handsomely, for it's the well-trained who find themselves mature in their relationship with God.

—Hebrews 12:4–11 *The Message*

CAMPING AND WARRIOR TALKS

"Daddy, I'm not sure what to do about this. . . . I think there are some girls who like me. How do I handle that?" Brennan, my son, shared those words around a recent campfire that was part of a father-son campout. We refer to these campfires as "warrior talks," times I gather with my sons to have conversation about a man's journey with God. And this one was a memorable one.

It began with an invitation—"Hey guys, do you want to go camping this week?" The question alone made my two oldest sons'—Caleb's and Brennan's—eyes sparkle and hearts come alive. Oh, the thrill of camping for a young boy. Invitation accepted . . . we began to make plans for our adventure. The location would be a local state park. Fishing would be on the agenda, along with swimming and playing in the woods. An adventure like this would also involve the search for a dangerous snake or wild bear. I talked with them about some of the hard stuff we would do in addition to the fun activities. They would have to help me set up camp, gather firewood, and then tear down camp before departing. There would also be some challenges/ tests involved in the camping adventure. They would need to prove their strength and overcome.

The day came for us to load the Jeep and head out on our adventure. The boys helped me load the trailer with sleeping bags, a tent, firewood, flashlights, lanterns, food, a cooler with drinks, cots, BB guns, fishing poles, tackle boxes, worms, crickets, chairs, matches, an axe, and a shovel. As you can tell, our packing list was quite simple! Packing was part of the adventure. Was it work? Sure it was . . . it takes a lot of work to go camping. But as we packed, I could see the excitement building in the boys' eyes. They could not wait to get out in the wild.

We arrived at the state park and picked our campsite. After parking, we began the unloading process. The boys were ready to jump in the lake or go fishing, but I had to force them to unload. And I do mean *force*. The complaining quickly started . . . "This is too heavy." "I'm tired." "Why do we have to do this?" "Can't we get to the fun stuff?" "Come on, Dad, this is boring." "I'm thirsty." "Geez." And the complaints continued throughout the unloading process.

We finally got camp set up and were off to the lake for a swim. The beach area by the lake was vacant, and we quickly dove in and cooled off from the beating rays of the hot sun. Boys, though, are not OK with a relaxing swim in the lake. There must be competition. There must be a test. We raced to the boundary ropes surrounding the swimming area. We threw rocks at a pipe to try and see who could hit it. We swam around looking for snakes or fish. Suddenly, Brennan yelled, "Guys, look at this, I found a turtle." It was about the size of a nickel . . . the tiniest turtle I had ever seen. But it was now a captured turtle. The little guy became our camping pet. We found a bucket to put him in and created living space to include rocks, grass, and an inch of water.

Our adventures continued with fishing that evening. Once again, with boys, fishing is not a relaxing way of taking in nature's elements and enjoying the sunset. There is a drive to catch the "big one." We fished for a few hours, caught some brim, and found ourselves exploring along the banks. And then suddenly around sunset, a giant (at least to us) water moccasin appeared. It slithered along the water bank and finally coiled up in a spot just beyond my feet. I have to admit, I was shaking in my tennis shoes as I looked down to discover the elongated reptile looking right at me in his coiled state. The boys gathered around, hearts beating faster than a kid in a dentist chair, and we devised a plan to take him out. We found a small boulder and decided we would drop it on him and then run. I dropped the massive rock, missed him by a few inches, and then we ran. It was dangerous, and we loved it.

That night, the boys gathered up some firewood, and I walked them through the proper ways to build and manage a fire. (Yes, I finally learned to properly build a fire!) We cooked hot dogs, ate potato chips, and drank some caffeinated soft drinks. We topped the meal off with s'mores . . . chocolate and marshmallows melted between two graham crackers. Yum!

After dinner, it was time for warrior talks. It was not a formal transition from s'mores to conversation around the fire. It just happened . . . naturally. I began to talk to the boys about a man's heart, a man's journey. We discussed everything—God, girls, shooting guns, cussing, sex, marriage, beer, and girls once again . . . the popular topic of the night. It was in the context of this talk that Brennan's question came out . . . "Daddy, I'm not sure what to do about this. . . . I think there are some girls who like me. How do I handle that?" Those words flowing out a young man's mouth were both heartwarming and hilarious. Caleb and I looked at each other and chuckled under our breaths. It was such an honest, candid question. I looked at Caleb and said, "What do you think about that? What should Brennan do?" This gave Caleb a chance to assert some strength and be a great brother. I cannot remember his exact response, but it alluded to being careful with girls and not getting tied down too early with one girl. What a moment!

Our talk lasted for a few hours. It was natural, not forced. It was friendly conversation more than a classroom lecture. It created space for us to talk about the real pressures of life. Our relationships with each other and with God matured that night. And the warrior talks around the campfire continue to this day. Sometimes they happen in the backyard around the fire pit and other times at a local restaurant or on camping adventures.

As yawns filled the late-night air, we settled into our tent for a good night's rest. The next morning, we swam again coupled with another round of fishing to bring our time of adventure to a close. It was now time to break camp, clean up, and load the trailer for our journey home.

One night . . . filled with adventure, danger, fun, work, and great conversation.

Whether it was camping or sports or hanging out in the backyard, did you ever have time like this with your dad? If so, describe it. If not, do you wish you would have?

For fathers with sons, describe a recent adventure together. And have you been able to have heart-to-heart conversations (warrior talks) with your son?

DISCIPLINE

What are the first few words that come to mind when you think of discipline?

For me, I tend to think of words like *duty*, *harsh*, *obligation*, *pain*, and *focus*. And those words certainly describe discipline. We might even think of an athlete who is disciplined when training for an event or race. We may think of a student who is disciplined in study when preparing for a test. Or we may also have images of a parent disciplining a child for a wrong behavior.

This chapter highlights the fourth phase of a man's journey with God in restoration. We began with the two phases of knowing God as Father and knowing self. These are foundational and must be revisited continually in a man's life. The previous phase dealt with living in brokenness and humility. We looked at the biblical theme and truth that God demonstrates His power and restoration in the weak, the broken. Instead of hiding or denying our brokenness, we are called as men to be open about our brokenness, our sin, and our struggles . . . with God and with others. This allows and invites God to do a work of healing and restoration.

And now we come to the fourth and final phase. It deals with how we walk with God in the disciplines. The goal of this chapter is to connect the disciplines with the fathering heart of God. Basically, we are linking this phase with the first one . . . knowing God as Father. The disciplines are avenues of fathering.

Let that statement soak in for a minute . . . *the disciplines are avenues of fathering*. They provide ways for us to know God, walk with God, and grow in relationship with Him. A disciplined man is a fathered man. The disciplines put us in a place or a posture to be fathered by God.

Have you thought of disciplines like prayer, Bible reading, or confession in this way?

CAMPING AND THE DISCIPLINES

Camping with my sons involved a lot of different activities and challenges. It also involved discipline, testing, and proving. I intentionally planned some difficult things to challenge them. Initiation comes when a man is tested. Masculinity is something that needs to be proven and called forth. But the goal of our campout was not to be disciplined or to learn how to be a good scout. The goal wasn't to win the challenge or come out on top with the biggest fish. The goal was time together. The goal was the maturing of a father-son relationship.

Relationship is central when it comes to the disciplines. The goal is not for you, as a man, to become more disciplined. The goal is not for you to learn how to be a "good Christian." The goal is not for you to win every challenge you face and be successful for God. The goal of practicing the disciplines (such as prayer or Bible reading) is time with God and growth in a father-son relationship.

Relating to God as a good father releases the pressure in our attempts to try harder and become more disciplined. We sometimes think we have to figure this Christian thing out and that our disciplined life will make us "right" with God. That could not be further from the truth of grace. The disciplines put us in a place to receive and to be fathered. The point is not the disciplines; the point is relationship. A disciplined man is a free man, a fathered man.

Richard Foster, in his book *Celebration of Discipline,* refers to the disciplines as the "door to liberation." The disciplines give us the opportunity to become "deep people" who experience the extraordinary power of God in our ordinary lives.[28] Marjorie Thompson refers to the disciplines as garden tools that create the best opportunity for growth. While not responsible for growth, the tools/disciplines help the soil of our hearts remain open to growth in relationship.[29] Dallas Willard reminds us that the disciplines are far more than something we do. They are related to a life where we are experiencing more of God on a daily basis. The disciplines allow His life to be poured into our lives.[30]

My goal during camping was to create a bond between my sons and me. They may or may not remember all the details from the adventure. They may or may not remember how to build a fire, set up a tent, or kill a water moccasin (or throw a rock at it and run), but I hope they are closer to me now than before. I hope our relationship is stronger because of the planned time together.

Disciplines are avenues of fathering. They give us the opportunity to walk with God, experience His presence, draw strength in our weakness, and be restored on a daily basis.

There are a lot of disciplines that could be highlighted in this chapter. We will focus on four. Two of the disciplines should come as little to no surprise—Bible reading and prayer. But seeing these two disciplines through the lens of fathering will open a new world in your life as a man. The other two may be new to your thinking on disciplines—warfare and confession.

---

[28]Richard Foster, *Celebration of Discipline: The Path to Spiritual Growth* (New York: HarperCollins, 1998).

[29]Marjorie J. Thompson, *Soul Feast: An Invitation to the Christian Spiritual Life* (Louisville: John Knox Press, 2014), 10–11.

[30]Dallas Willard, *The Spirit of the Disciplines*: *Understanding How God Changes Lives* (New York: Harper Collins, 1988).

DISCIPLINE/AVENUE OF FATHERING #1: BIBLE READING

Let's begin with our first discipline, reading the Bible. The Bible is primary when it comes to a relationship with God. We have studied various passages of Scripture throughout this process to give us an understanding of God and ourselves. In chapter 2, we looked at God as Father and studied Luke 15. Hopefully, God spoke to your heart through His Word and revealed His image and His ways as Father. We focused on knowing self in chapter 3 as we explored the life of David and applied his journey to our own. We quickly saw that our emotional lives and stories cannot be separated from our spiritual lives. For example, what a man does with his anger is in direct relation to his walk with God. They cannot be separated. God speaks to us in both head and heart, redeeming both intellect and emotions. Chapter 4 dealt with three significant passages on how God restores broken men—Psalm 51, Hosea 2, and 2 Corinthians 12. We were able to see how God reveals His power in the depths of our weakness. What a powerful truth from the Bible.

The Bible is not a secondary or secular document that functions as an appendage to the Christian life. It is primary and it is central. We rely on God's Word as the primary way that God speaks to and guides us and fathers us. He can certainly speak in other ways, such as through prayer and through community. But everything is built on the foundation of His speaking through the Bible.

Have you seen, thus far, how God has been speaking and fathering through the Bible, His Holy Word?

What is your relationship with the Bible?

Growing up, how did you view the Bible?

How did your dad handle the Bible? Your mom?

How would you like to grow when it comes to the Bible?

Instead of merely talking about the discipline of Bible reading, we will now walk through a quick exercise on reading the Bible as a way for God to father us as men. Here is what the movement looks like: pray, meditate, apply, and pray.

Pray

Begin by talking with God and inviting Him to speak to you through His Word.

"Father, I bring all of myself to You today. I lay aside the many distractions screaming for my attention. Clear my mind, now, as

I read and listen. Would You speak, and would You father me? I belong to You, and I choose to listen as You speak to my heart."

Put this prayer in your own words . . . no need to be lengthy. Beginning with prayer helps you be in a posture of listening and invites God to speak to you.

Meditate

Reread Hebrews 12:4–11 from the beginning of this chapter. Read slowly, and read it a few times.

Write down the primary truths from the passage. Jot down the phrases that stand out to you.

What is God revealing about Himself in this passage?

What does this passage reveal about you?

What does this passage reveal about the ways God fathers a man?

Apply

We have prayed, asking God to speak through the Bible. We have now meditated on the passage from Hebrews and identified major truths about God, us, and how He fathers. Now, we come to the application. This is vital to reading Scripture. Knowledge must always lead to application of truth.

Based on the truths you found in Hebrews 12:4–11, how are you being invited to live in response?

Think about some current situations, problems, struggles, or doubts in your life. How is God speaking to you about those situations or relationships?

Pray

We bring the time to a close by having more conversation with God about what His Word has revealed.

"Father, thank You for the truth and power of Your Word. [I am struggling in my job and my future at this company. I am frustrated about my marriage . . . seems like we are walking through a wilderness right now.] I bring those things to You. Your word from Hebrews reminds me today that You are fathering me and disciplining me out of love. You are exposing parts of me that need to grow. You are revealing some of my sin and brokenness. I bring all that to You. I choose to live in trust today. I acknowledge that You are in control over [my job/my marriage/etc.]. Give me Your strength today."

Once again, put this prayer in your own words. Make it a conversation with God that drives the truths from Scripture into your heart and responds to what He has revealed.

The pray, meditate, apply, and pray exercise can be done in a few minutes or, if time allows, be given a greater allotment of time. More than a method, it is a way of listening to God through the Bible. Remember, the discipline of reading and listening to God's Word is a discipline, an avenue for God to father you as a son.

DISCIPLINE/AVENUE OF FATHERING #2: PRAYER

The next discipline to explore is prayer. Much of the previous discipline led us through some time of prayer and having conversation with God. In simple terms, prayer is conversation with God. Conversations involve two-way dialogue. Sometimes, prayer can be viewed as monologue . . . our talks with Him. It is healthier to see it as a conversation, a way of growing closer to Him.

The warrior talks with my sons around the campfire were conversations. Yes, I did have some specific things I wanted to talk about with Caleb and Brennan, but it was a chance for us to share concerns, laughter, questions, and fears around the campfire. We had conversation where they listened while also offering up some questions and statements from their own hearts. At its core, that's prayer—conversation that involves God speaking to you and your honest response, questions, or statements back to Him.

Let's practice the discipline of prayer right now. You can pray out loud or pray quietly. You can also write out a prayer. I find writing my prayers sometimes helps me focus and listen. A lot of times God will even speak as I'm writing or praying. This is just an example. Use your own words:

> Father, I've been doing a lot of thinking about life. Seems I'm doing a lot of looking back and looking forward. I look back with a lot of regrets and wish I could redo some things. I look forward with some anxiety about what's next. Some of my worries center around finances, my kids, my wife, and my career. My heart is kind of unsettled today as I pray. I am just reminded right now that You are my Father. I am reminded that You are the One writing my story, and You are fathering me. You use the weak, broken parts of my life to grow me, restore me, and strengthen me. I do ask for clarity about what's next in my life. I ask for You to help me love my wife and children well. I belong to You . . . guide me and father me today. Amen.

Similar to the campfire, isn't it? Natural, not forced. More of a friendly conversation than a classroom lecture. The discipline of prayer is a way to have conversation with God and is an avenue of fathering in your life.

Take some time to pray and talk with God. If it helps, write out a prayer and see if God speaks to you/fathers you through the discipline of prayer.

DISCIPLINE/AVENUE OF FATHERING #3: WARFARE

The next two disciplines—warfare and confession—may not be as familiar to you as Bible reading and prayer. Over the years, I have seen many men come alive in relationship with God by exercising these two disciplines. And we rarely see these as avenues of fathering.

Let's look at the discipline of warfare as a way for God to father us as men. Warfare assumes a few things. It assumes we are in a battle, that we have an enemy, and that we have a role to play. First, we are in a battle. Paul reminds us in Ephesians 6 that our battle is not against flesh and blood but against powers of the dark world and forces of evil (v. 12). Many Christian men live as though there is no battle. If there is a battle taking place, then things like prayer become vital weapons for us. Second, we have an enemy. Satan is opposed to God and to those who belong to God, His children. That's me and that's you. Do you and I live as though we have an enemy? Do our prayers reflect a belief that we are being opposed by one who likes to steal, kill, and destroy (see John 10:10)? We must remember on a daily basis that we have an enemy. And third, we have a role to play. God is the only One who can overcome the attacks from our enemy, but He works through us. Our prayers matter. How we live matters. And we have been given the power and authority of Christ to overcome the enemy.

How can we view warfare as a discipline, an avenue of fathering? Here's the short answer. You are being opposed right now. The enemy is using distraction, fear, worry, temptation, lust, hatred, and more to wreak havoc on your life. Satan also uses religion, hypocrisy, and denial to lull us into thinking he does not exist. So you are in a battle. How does a soldier know their training and preparations are adequate? Not in a boardroom but in battle. God has you on the battlefield of life right now, and He knows everything you are going through. He is training and initiating you as a son in the battle. He is training your masculine, warrior heart in the midst of the battle.

Warfare, then, is not merely an exercise in overcoming the powers of darkness. There's a greater truth going on here. Warfare is where you are being fathered. Warfare is more about God than about the enemy. He is strengthening you, restoring you, and maturing you in the midst of the battle, suffering, and hardship.

What a change of perspective! Think about it.

How different would it be if you viewed warfare as a discipline, an avenue for God to father you?

Today, right now, where are you facing warfare? (thoughts, job, relationships, trust, money, etc.)

How different would your day look if you knew the warfare, the enemy's opposition, was actually a discipline God was using to father you? Give some practical answers.

DISCIPLINE/AVENUE OF FATHERING #4: CONFESSION

The last discipline we will look at is confession. To confess is to acknowledge brokenness and dependence. It takes us back to chapter 4, "Live in Brokenness and Humility." Confession is vital to brokenness, which leads to restoration. If you want to live in the restorative power of Christ, then practice the discipline of confession. If your church, small group, or men's group wants to live in the restorative power of Christ, then we must practice the discipline of confession.

Confession helps us fight against the temptation to hide or live in denial. There is much about human nature that wants to cover weakness. It is particularly natural for Americans, struggling with individualism, to hide our brokenness. The call and invitation for Christian men is to practice confession, which means to be open about our hurts, weaknesses, pain, struggles, and sin. To confess is to agree that we are a broken and dependent people.

Confession is to be practiced with God and with others. With God, our prayers should be confessional, in that they are filled with openness, honesty, and transparency. You might ask, "Well, doesn't God already know my weaknesses?" Yes He does, but there is power in confessing and bringing those things out into the open with God. It does wonders for our hearts to confess. We are also invited to experience confession with others. This is where community comes into play. Whether with one person or a small group of trusted friends, confession draws us closer and allows the power of God to work through us. If you are walking with a group of men right now, confession will be primary to shaping an honest, open culture. When you confess, it gives others the opportunity to bring their brokenness before the God who restores.

Confession is a discipline, an avenue of fathering. God fathers through confession. What a gift from our loving Father! When we stand in agreement and confess our brokenness, weakness, and struggles, God meets us there. He steps in and fathers us, leading us through the process of restoration. Instead of running away, He draws close to the broken. Luke 15, the prodigal's story, reminds us that "when he came to his senses"— that's confession— his journey home began, and he was welcomed with open, loving arms. That's available to you and to me.

In your own words, how is confession an avenue of fathering?

What fears do you have about practicing confession with God?

What fears do you have about practicing confession with others?

Will you choose to practice the discipline of confession or at least ask God to show you more about this discipline?

If you are walking with a group of men, I encourage you to look at the appendix section titled, Check-Ins, which provide a way to practice confession with a group of men.

Chapter 6

THE JOURNEY AHEAD

"Well, son, we've done it. Daisy's restoration is finished. This race car is ready to race again. A lot of work, a lot of time, and a lot of relationship building. Definitely worth it."

Still polishing up the hood, you speak up, "Whew, you've got that right, Grandpa. A lot of work. But look at this beauty now! To be honest, when I saw Daisy down in the barn I never knew she could look this good again." Tossing the polishing cloth to the side, you ask, "What's next?"

Grandpa moves to the back of the shiny, restored race car, "Let's push her out. Why don't you get back here with me and let's gently walk her out."

Together, you and Grandpa move the race car out of the garage and onto the rocky path out front. Holding up a shiny key and tossing it your way, Grandpa says, "All right, son, you know what's next. Why don't you take Daisy for a spin?"

Eyes lighting up, head tilted a bit, "Really? You mean I can drive her around? Yes!"

"Well, that is why we restored this car, isn't it? No need to just look at it or let it sit in this old garage. Hop in."

You climb into the race car and start it up. Engine humming, you sit there filled with a mixture of exhilaration and fulfillment. Thinking to yourself, "Wow, my dad once sat in this same driver's seat. And here I am . . . today . . . taking this car, Dad's car, Grandpa's car, for a drive."

Grandpa steps up to the window, leans down, and says, "Proud of you, son. You did it . . . we did it. Now enjoy the ride!"

With that, you speed off. A restored man driving a restored race car.

Now to Him who is able to do immeasurably more than all we ask or imagine, according to His power that is at work within us, to Him be the glory in the church and in Christ Jesus through all generations, for ever and ever! Amen.

—Ephesians 3:20–21

THE CHRISTMAS OF MORE

It was Christmas 1982. And yes, I realize I am dating myself by mentioning that year. We were living in Thomaston, Georgia, and my dad was the pastor of a small Baptist church. Christmas, in the post-Santa Claus years, involved my parents' unique way of wrapping gifts and whetting our appetite. My dad was the king of wrapping gifts in a mysterious way. He would place various items like marbles or bricks in the boxes prior to wrapping. When we would shake the box, we could never figure it out. The gifts would be placed out a few weeks before Christmas, which drove us crazy. We begged each night before Christmas . . . *Can we open just one gift tonight? Please?*

And then, finally, the sacred day arrived . . . Christmas morning. The time when we were able to open presents and see what surprises awaited us. Christmas of 1982 unfolded in that usual sort of way. All of the gifts were opened and the noise of four wild boys filled the room. Suddenly, a hush filled the room when my parents announced . . . "But wait, there's more!"

What a statement. Whether it's one more gift on your birthday, one more elaborate aspect to your meal, or one more announcement from your boss who just offered you a raise, you can feel the anticipation and excitement build.

And that is what filled our hearts as they scurried off to their bedroom. They returned holding the amazing, long-awaited . . . Atari

Video Computer System. Before there was Nintendo, PlayStation, Kindle, or iPad . . . there was Atari. The MacDaddy of game systems with its rectangular, black box, various game cartridges, two game controllers with long cords, and the infamous joystick. I can still remember playing *Frogger* into the wee hours of the night. It was the Christmas of *more*.

We have reached the final chapter in the Restored Man process. You have trekked through the four phases: know God as Father, know self, live in brokenness and humility, and walk with God in the disciplines. You have spent plenty of time wrestling with the deep issues of your masculine heart. You have ventured back into your story, identifying wounds or places of stuck-ness. You have experienced God's restorative power in the midst of your weakness. You have done well, my brother.

But wait, there's more. That is the call of this final chapter . . . the journey ahead. There's more, a lot more, for you to experience in your journey as a man with God. We have merely begun to see the intricacies and depths of a father-relationship with God, made possible through the life and work of Jesus Christ and present in the restorative work of the Holy Spirit. There is so much more that God wants to do in your life.

GOING BACK TO GO FORWARD

A slingshot provides a fitting metaphor for this section. A rock nestled in the pocket of the sling contains potential power. But it is only in being pulled back that it is able to be launched forward. Let's go back and revisit the four phases of the Restored Man process. Here are a few questions to help us remember where we have been. See how much you can answer without turning back to those chapters. Afterward, feel free to turn back and check your answers.

Phase #1: Know God as Father

How does a man's relationship with his earthly dad affect his view of or relationship with God?

What is one theme that stands out about your relationship with your earthly father?

What does Luke 15, the parable of the loving father and the two sons, reveal about the heart of God as Father?

What practical differences come in a man's journey when God fathers him on a daily basis?

Phase #2: Know Self

Why is it important for a man to spend time working back through his story?

Can you identify a theme or two from your story that continues to affect you today?

We spent a good bit of time working through King David's story. Do you recall a scene or two that stood out? Why?

What are some practical implications of spending time working through your own story? How could this affect a man's relationships, job, or walk with God?

Phase #3: Live in Brokenness and Humility

Put this theme from the Bible in your own words: God demonstrates His power through broken, weak people.

We looked at Psalm 51 (David's response of brokenness after adultery and murder), Hosea 2 (God's restorative pursuit of Gomer through Hosea), and 2 Corinthians 12 (God's demonstration of power in Paul's weakness/thorn). Which one stands out to you and why?

What hinders you from living in brokenness and vulnerability on a daily basis?

What are the practical implications in a man's life if he chooses to live daily in brokenness and vulnerability?

Phase #4: Walk with God in the Disciplines

Disciplines are avenues of fathering. Do you view the disciplines (such as Bible reading and prayer) differently from when you began this process? If so, how?

Warfare is one of the ways God disciples and fathers us. Why is it important for a man to realize there is a battle taking place every day? And how does it help to see warfare as an avenue of God's fathering?

Confession was the final discipline we explored. In the context of a relationship with God, why is confession important? And in the context of community with other men, why is confession important?

Two Final Questions:

How has the Restored Man process affected your relationship with God and others? If married, how has it affected your marriage?

Now that you have finished the journey, what are some important next steps to continue growth?

Christmas 1982 will forever be remembered as the Christmas of *more*. The Atari game system made it a memorable holiday. There's nothing like hearing the words, "But wait . . . there's more!" As the closing credits hit the screen on this journey together, this is my prayer for you and for me, as sons of the Father:

> Now Father, You have been present throughout this process. You have spoken to my brother and fathered him through the pages of *The Restored Man*. You have revealed the faulty images we have of You and replaced those with truth. You have taken us back in our stories to unearth broken, sinful scenes. All done for the purpose of restoration. You have invited us to live in brokenness and vulnerability with You and others. And You continue to father us through the disciplines of the Christian life. You are worthy of a life well lived. You are the God of immeasurably more. Show us the next steps and continue the work of fathering our masculine hearts. You alone deserve the praise and glory. Amen . . . in agreement with my brother, my restored brother!

Here are the keys . . . enjoy the ride!

Appendix

STARTING YOUR RESTORED MAN GROUP

The Restored Man is a resource for individuals and groups. I would encourage you to work through this resource individually first. A man cannot lead a group to a place he has not visited. If led to take a group of men through the Restored Man process, I want to provide some structure to help you facilitate a group.

Top 10 Ways to Shut Down a Men's Group

1. Use lots of religious clichés.
2. In the first meeting, ask the men to share their deepest and darkest secret.
3. Speak 90 percent of the time, allowing only for minor discussion points.
4. Make the meeting overly formal with a minute-by-minute agenda.
5. Have the men sit in rows instead of a circle.
6. In the first meeting, instead of sharing personal struggles, talk about how you are doing great and have figured out the perfect relationship with God.
7. Begin each meeting with one hour of prayer requests so the guys can talk about everything except what is most needed.
8. Provide a thick binder filled with pages of notes and handouts along with a course evaluation.
9. Speak in second person (you) more than first person (I).
10. If needed, and I doubt you will, repeat the first nine steps until your men's group shuts down.

Top 10 Ways to Lead a Restored Man Group

1. Allow the first few meetings to be get-to-know-you meetings. Don't get too heavy with topics unless the men are willing to go there.

2. Food or snacks help set the tone for fellowship and relaxation. You want men to feel comfortable when coming to the group.

3. The location of your group may take place in a home, at work, or at church. No matter the location, try to make it feel comfortable and less formal.

4. Have the guys sit in a circle or around a table. If in a home, couches are perfect.

5. Balance structure and freedom. Avoid being legalistic about time and your agenda. At the same time, use the Group Guide, and have a plan for your meeting. The more you meet, the less you will need to follow a strict outline.

6. Try to plan a few outings, if possible. Whether a night of bowling, a firepit, or outdoor activity, relationships will be strengthened through being together in a "non-group" setting.

7. Share and model transparency in the group. Men will follow your lead. If you share little, they will share little. But if you open up about your own life and story, they will follow your example.

8. Find ways to help men connect between meetings. Whether through a group text or through social media, find ways to help the men build relationships between meetings.

9. Have a beginning and end date. Have a beginning and end time. Men like to know what they are committing to. As you meet and men begin to open up, you may see the need to adjust the time allotment for the meeting.

10. Pray and lead from your heart. The greatest thing men need is a group of brothers. You have the opportunity to breathe life and freedom and restoration into another man's heart—what a privilege . . . and what a responsibility. Lead from your heart.

TEN-WEEK GROUP GUIDE FOR ORGANIZING YOUR MEETING

Meeting #1

Introduction and Desire

The goal for your group's first meeting is to build relationships and set the tone for ten weeks together. The early meetings of your group are vital to create a culture of honesty and acceptance. As you meet, and men build trust, this will come more naturally.

Opening Fellowship and Food

Give the men some time to eat and share. This will help the group feel more at home during your first meeting.

Opening Check-In

Be sure to read over appendix item titled Check-Ins to become familiar with the best ways to do a check-in. It is helpful to begin most of your meetings with some type of check-in. For the first meeting, begin with a basic check-in:

- What is your name?
- Share about your family.
- Share about your job and what you do during the week.
- What excites you about beginning with this group?
- What makes you anxious about beginning with this group?

"You Are Here" Check-In

Now the men have shared some basic information about themselves, you can move to the "You Are Here" Check-In, which allows for more in-depth sharing.

- On the road of life, which image best matches where you are? (Feel free to create your own description or elaborate on the provided descriptions.)

    Cruising along on the highway of life

    Broken down on the side of the road

    Lost in the middle of nowhere

    Driving but in need of some direction

- How would you describe your current relationship with God?

- What seems to be missing or what would you like to grow in?

- On a scale of 1 to 10, with 1 being not connected at all and 10 being in constant connection, how connected are you with God?

- If you are married, on a scale of 1 to 10, with 1 being not connected at all and 10 being in constant connection, how connected are you with your wife? Feel free to elaborate.

- What do you most desire from this community of men?

- What do you most desire from this process in the coming weeks?

Restored Man Group Covenant

Have the men look over the My Restored Man Group Covenant in the appendix. You can also find a digital version at www.therestoredman .com if you want to print the covenant or share it through email. Whether you have each man sign it or make a verbal commitment, men want to know what is expected. Go through the covenant in detail and have the group share their contact information with one another.

Looking Ahead: Week 2

In the coming week, there are two reminders to give to the group. First, encourage them to share in between meetings if they have a need. It may take some time for the men to open up, but be sure to encourage the sharing of personal needs. You can model sharing needs by sending out personal communication during the week.

Second, encourage the men to work through the introduction, "Men, Something Is Missing," and chapter 1, "Starting Point: Why Do This?" Chapter 1 has three assessments to be completed this week:

- An Exercise in Desire
- Self-Assessment
- Spouse and/or Friend Assessment

Digital versions of these assessments can be found at www.therestoredman.com. Encourage your group to spend time completing each assessment, and ask them to bring them to the following meeting.

Final Word and Prayer

It will probably be best for you to give some final words and lead in prayer. In future weeks, if a man is comfortable praying, you may want to ask others to pray.

Meeting #2: Starting Point

Opening Fellowship and Food

Whether you provide food and drinks weekly, it is important to have this in the early weeks to create a relaxing environment.

Opening Check-In: Desire

Hopefully each man was able to answer the questions in the section "An Exercise in Desire." Allow time to talk through some of the questions about personal growth and/or relationship/marriage growth.

Check-In: Assessments

Point the men to the self-assessment in chapter 1, "Starting Point." You may even want to allow a few minutes for men to complete the assessment and/or look over their answers. Some men may not feel comfortable sharing their results, but we want to create space for those who are ready to share. Have the men share their lowest scoring category from the four phases: Know God as Father, Know Self, Live in Brokenness and Humility, and Walk with God in the Disciplines.

If any of the men have their results of the Wife/Friend Assessment and would be willing to share, allow some time to do so.

The goal of the assessments is to create a baseline for growth. This is not a legalistic tool to highlight failure. Carefully walk through these, and encourage the men to set some goals for growth in their lower scoring areas. It is simply a tool, not a report card on their life.

Looking Ahead: Week 3

Hopefully, by the end of the second meeting, your group has been able to build some level of trust while completing the introduction and chapter 1. In the coming week, ask the men to read and work through the questions in chapter 2, "Know God as Father." We will spend two weeks on this phase of *The Restored Man*, but challenge the men to work through as much as possible in the coming week.

Meetings 3 and 4: Know God as Father

From here on out, I encourage you to take two weeks to go through the following chapters to adequately cover each phase of the Restored Man process. Meetings three and four will focus on phase 1: Know God as Father.

Opening Food and Fellowship

As we noted earlier, this is encouraged to build a comfortable environment for your meetings. Providing food is at the leader's discretion.

Opening Check-In

Choose from the following open-ended discussion questions to begin each of these meetings:

- Share a fun memory or adventure you had with your father.
- What was a favorite hobby or sport your father enjoyed?
- What is one way you wanted to be like your father?
- For the fathers in the group, what do you most enjoy about being a dad?

Going Deeper Check-In

Reference the list of father questions from phase 1: Know God as Father, and encourage the men to share:

- What words did you list to describe your father?
- How did your dad handle emotions like anger, sadness, or grief?
- What is one positive characteristic you gained from your relationship with your father?
- What is one thing you wish you had experienced or heard from your father?
- On the scale of characteristics, which mark is farthest to the right? Can you explain or give an example of this characteristic in your father's life?
- How has your relationship with your earthly father affected your relationship with God, your Heavenly father?

Knowing God as Father

Reference the section on the Prodigal's Father from Luke 15.

- What is the primary theme from this story in Luke 15?
- How much are you like the younger brother?

- How much are you like the older brother?
- What did you learn about yourself through studying Luke 15 and answering the questions in this section?
- In your own words, what does it mean to know God as a Father? What is one way this could affect your relationship with God?

Looking Ahead

As you finish your third meeting, be sure to encourage the men to spend some time reviewing or finishing Phase 1: Know God as Father. Also encourage them to make some connections with each other through the week, between meetings.

In meeting three or four, it would be helpful to plan an outing or adventure together for the coming weeks. Whether an outdoor adventure, bowling night, or firepit (just a few examples), have the men share ideas for a group gathering.

As you finish your fourth meeting, encourage the men to begin work on chapter 3: "Know Self." This chapter is an exploration in King David's life and your life as a man. Encourage the men to block out some time during their week to read and answer the questions from each section.

Meetings 5 and 6: Know Self

Your group has probably moved beyond the "get to know you" stage. By these meetings, there should be some level of trust and transparency in the group. You may also want to revisit the Restored Man Covenant as a reminder for the group's purpose and goals of trust, open-sharing, and confidentiality. Be sure to model these qualities in how you lead the group.

Opening Check-In

As the men gather, choose from the following open-ended discussion questions.

- Are you enjoying the story of the grandson and his grandfather restoring a car at the beginning of each chapter? Have you ever wanted to restore an old car? If so, what would you want to restore/rebuild?
- Did you have a grandfather growing up? Describe a positive memory you have of your relationship with him.
- From the "Know Your Beginnings" section, tell us about where you grew up. Do you have a fun story from childhood?
- From the "Know Your Friendships" section, who were your closest friends as a boy? Was your connection through sports, school, hobbies, activities, etc.?

Going Deeper Check-In

After the men settle into the meeting and feel more comfortable, you can go deeper with questions from the "Know Your Sexual Story" or "Know Your Grief" sections. Your leadership through these questions is vital. There is no need to avoid the tough or uneasy questions. You can model transparency by sharing some of your answers to the questions. While you do not want to call on men to share, you may want to encourage men to share openly and listen attentively. Remember the group covenant; we are not here to fix a man but to be a good brother and good listener.

- How did you father handle sexual topics?
- Did your family talk about sexual matters or avoid sexual matters?
- What do you wish had been provided for you, as a young boy/man, to help you handle sexual matters/struggles?
- How did you feel alone in trying to figure out sex, girls, and relationships?
- What were some of your losses as a young boy/man? From elementary school years? From your teen years?

- How did your father handle grief/loss? How did your mother handle grief/loss?
- How would a close friend say you deal with losses/setbacks/grief?
- In working through your story and phase 2: Know Self, what is one thing you learned about yourself?

King David's Story

One of the goals of phase 2: Know Self is to learn about a central figure in the Old Testament. Much has been written about King David's life. His life parallels many parts of a man's journey. Ask the men to look over the chapter and share one highlight from David's life. Help relate each highlight from David's story to a man's journey with God.

Looking Ahead

As you finish meeting five, encourage the men to review or complete phase 2: Know Self. This is an important section that typically takes a few weeks to finish. Challenge the men to block out some time this week to walk with God and work through the questions.

After finishing phase 2: Know Self and both meetings five and six, the men will have shared much from their stories. The group should be feeling more like a band of brothers than merely a men's group. The past few weeks have also required a good bit of emotional energy. This would be a great point in the group's journey to do a fun activity allowing for laughter and adventure together.

As you finish meeting six, encourage the men to begin work on chapter 4, "Live in Brokenness and Humility."

Meetings 7 and 8: Live in Brokenness and Humility

Opening Check-In

Chapter 4, "Live in Brokenness and Humility," begins with a story from my childhood about G.I. Joe going up in flames. Have some of the men in your group share stories of adventure from their childhood. From wild adventures to battles, there are certain to be some fun and "dangerous" stories.

- How have you seen the truth, "Every man wants to be powerful," in your own life or in boys' lives?
- What were some of your childhood heroes and/or superheroes?
- Why are boys drawn to images of being powerful?
- What does that say about a man's heart and desires?
- What does the world say is required for a man to be powerful?
- When you hear "live in brokenness and humility," what comes to mind?

Going Deeper Check-In: Biblical Theme of Power in Weakness
In the biblical overview, we said that the "weak" are containers for God's grace. God shows His power through lastborns, outcasts, misfits, physically broken people, and morally broken people.

- What frightens most men about revealing weakness to God, their spouse, or other men?
- Ask the group to state the biblical theme of living in brokenness and humility in their own words.

Going Deeper Check-In . . . The Three Steps
Spend some time in these meetings talking through the three steps of living in brokenness and humility. With each step, encourage and model applying each step in a personal and honest way.

Step 1: Admit Brokenness and Choose Humility (Psalm 51)

- What happened in David's life that led to the writing of this powerful psalm?
- How honest is David in this psalm? How does he practice confession with God?

- What is he asking God to do in his own life?
- With God's healing and power, what does David want to do for other broken men?
- **Confession**: In your own words, what does it mean for a man to confess and be open about his sin, struggles, and weaknesses?
- **Restoration**: God fathers and restores broken men. How would you describe a man who is being restored?
- **Leadership**: How has God used another person to encourage you? How might God want to use your life and story to encourage another man?

Step 2: Embrace God's Process for Restoration (Hosea 2)

- In the first part of Hosea 2 (verses 2–13), God exposes Gomer in her sin and adultery. In your own words, how is God's exposure an act of love?
- Why does God convict and highlight sin in our lives?
- Seeing God as our Father, how might this change the way you view conviction . . . instead of seeing it as punishment?
- As Hosea 2 continues, we see God doing a work of restoration in Gomer, Hosea, and in their marriage. Think about the theme of restoration we have highlighted through this process. Why is restoration such a beautiful image? Think about an old car being restored. Why does that tend to catch our attention? And why is it so powerful to see a man restored through brokenness and humility?

Step 3: Receive Power in Weakness (2 Corinthians 12)

- In 2 Corinthians 12, we spent some time exploring the thorn/ stake in Paul's life. What might this thorn/stake have been in Paul's life?
- Why would God allow a struggle, heartache, or burden in his life? In our lives?

- What does God say to Paul about how He will deliver power in his struggle, heartache, or burden?
- Are they any thorns/stakes (struggles, heartaches, or burdens) you have carried or are carrying?
- How might God want to deliver power and grace in your weakness?

Bringing It Home
A few questions to ask the group that will help personalize phase 3.

- How would living in brokenness and humility affect your relationship with God?
- If married, how would your marriage look different if you lived in brokenness and humility?
- How might others benefit from your weakness, instead of your "having it together"?

Meeting 9: Walk with God in the Disciplines

As your group enters the last two meetings, we return to covering one chapter per week. I pray that your group meetings have been instrumental in building brotherhood and growth among the men. Thank you for leading and pouring into these men. This chapter deals with disciplines as avenues or ways for God to father us. Here are some opening questions.

- What are the first few words that come to mind when you think of discipline?
- What difference might it make to think of disciplines, such as Bible study and prayer, as avenues of fathering?
- Take a few minutes to compare and contrast disciplines in a nonrelational way (going through the motions, duty, obligation, etc) versus in a relational way (avenues of fathering, relationship-focused, joyful, etc)?

Discipline/Avenue of Fathering #1: Bible Reading

- What is your relationship with the Bible?
- Growing up, how did you view the Bible?
- How did your dad handle the Bible? Your mom?
- How would you like to grow in seeing Bible reading as an avenue of God's fathering?

Discipline/Avenue of Fathering #2: Prayer

- How have you grown in prayer over the years?
- Where do you feel like a failure or inadequate when it comes to prayer?
- How would you like to grow in seeing prayer as an avenue of God's fathering?

Discipline/Avenue of Fathering #3: Warfare

- When you hear "spiritual warfare," what images or thoughts come to mind?
- What fears might men have about spiritual warfare?
- Where is the enemy, Satan, currently attacking or tempting you?
- How would you like to grow in seeing spiritual warfare as an avenue of God's fathering?

Discipline/Avenue of Fathering #4: Confession

- What fears do you have about practicing confession with God?
- What fears do you have about practicing confession with others?
- How might confession help draw men closer in relationships?
- How would you like to grow in seeing confession as an avenue of God's fathering?

As you finish meeting nine, encourage your group to finish strong as your study is close to completion. Ask the men to work on the final chapter, "The Journey Ahead," as you plan for the final meeting together.

Meeting 10: The Journey Ahead

As with all of your group's meetings, feel free to adjust any questions from the study guide to fit your group. A final meeting is a time to celebrate, look back, and talk about next steps. Here are some questions to guide your final meeting:

- In looking back at phase 1: Know God as Father, how does a man's relationship with his earthly dad affect his view of or relationship with God as Father?
- What practical differences come in a man's journey when he is being fathered by God daily?
- In looking back at phase 2: Know Self, why is it important for a man to spend time working back through his story? Can you identify a theme or two from your story that continues to affect you today? Is there a scene from King David's story that stands out to you?
- In looking back at phase 3: Live in Brokenness and Humility, put this theme—God demonstrates His power through broken, weak men—from the Bible in your own words. What hinders you from living in brokenness and humility on a daily basis? How might this strengthen a man's relationships (spouse, children, friends, coworkers, etc)?
- In looking back at phase 4: Walk with God in the Disciplines, how does it help a man to view disciplines (such as Bible reading and prayer) as avenues of fathering? How does it help a man to view spiritual warfare as a way for God to father and grow us? How does confession draw men closer in relationships?

As you near the end of meeting ten, share with the men in your group about next steps. What are one to two practical next steps that could be taken to continue growth in the Restored Man process?

MY RESTORED MAN GROUP COVENANT

In the first meeting, it is important to create a group covenant among the men, which helps build in expectation and accountability to the process. Your presence will be needed and your active engagement will be necessary. Be sure to get each man's info so you can reach out between meetings, if needed. It is also important to discuss the covenant guidelines below so everyone is in agreement. The group may feel free to add any additional guidelines.

Group Covenant:

Your presence is needed.
I will let my brothers know if I can't be at group.

Honesty is vital.
I commit to honesty with God and my brothers.

Work on my own heart.
I will work through *The Restored Man* as I walk with God.

We are not here to fix each other.
I commit to listen and pray for my brothers.

What is shared here stays here.
I respect confidentiality and trust with my brothers.

Name   Email   Cell Phone

_____

_____

_____

_____

_____

_____

_____

_____

_____

_____

_____

_____

_____

_____

CHECK-INS

Let me first introduce you to a check-in. Check-ins are vital to a men's group and the development of trust and community. Though not necessary to every group gathering, they should be a consistent part of the group meetings. Let me outline several components of a check-in:

A check-in should be personal . . . speak in first person. Our tendency, as men, is to talk in second or third person. Second person: "You know, sometimes you just feel confused or lost." Or "When you go through a hard time, you don't always know what to do." Third person: "My wife says she is tired of being disconnected." Or "There's a guy who says he struggles with being a dad and often feels like a failure." Instead of speaking in circles or masked language, it is much healthier for men to speak in first person when they check-in. For example: "I have had a difficult week at work, and I am unsure of my future at this company." Or "I am struggling in my marriage. I don't know what happened to the love we once had."

A check-in should involve facts** and **emotions** . . . **speak from your head and heart. "Just give me the facts" . . . that's a guy's way of getting to the bottom line. The problem with mere facts is that God has created us as logical and emotional beings. When we stick with the facts, we are slicing our lives in half. The facts are important to a check-in, but our emotions attached to the facts are equally important. Let me use the above examples to demonstrate: "I have had a difficult week at work, and I am unsure of my future at this company. I feel confused and angry about this situation." Or "I am struggling in my marriage. I don't know what happened to the love we once had. I am angry at myself over this and deeply sad that our marriage is so disconnected."

A check-in requires others to listen more than speak. We are fixers. As men, we want to step in, provide a solution, and get things moving forward. One of the ways to shut down a men's group and the desired transparency is to fix each other. Instead of letting a guy share and live in the unknowns, men want to provide a solution. When we do that, we treat a man's heart like a project to-do list at the local hardware store (by the way, we do this with our wives also . . . a woman does not want to be a project). When we fix, we try to play the role of God. When we listen and walk with a man in his present-tenseness, we learn the art of leaning on God and letting Him father us through life.

A check-in requires confidentiality and trust. Another cancer to a men's group is the uncertainty that "what's shared here, stays here" is not valued or followed. Men need to know the circle of brothers is a trusted circle. Anything shared in the group should remain in the trust of the community of men. This is vital to building trust and authenticity among the men. A man is free to share any personal growth or response from meeting but is not allowed to share another man's story, struggles, or concerns.

A check-in gives opportunity for all to share without letting anyone dominate discussion. It is important that each man is given an opportunity to share. Some men are more prone to open up and share than others. That may be due to personality or preference. The goal is to give each man a chance to provide a check-in. Some men may have more pressing issues or struggles. They may require more space and time to unpack their situation. That is certainly acceptable and desired. The caution is to not allow one man to dominate discussion or get the group off track.

Let me add one other quick note about check-ins. There is no need to be legalistic about how often check-ins should take place or how much of the group time should be taken by them. The general rule of thumb with a men's group is that a check-in should be a regular part of group meetings and a consistent way for men to listen and connect.

LOVING A WOMAN

(Excerpt from Randy and Melody's book *30 Days of Hope for Hurting Marriages*, available from New Hope Publishers.)

Here are eight quick thoughts on loving your wife:

1. Validation. This is foundational. Because of the brokenness of man stemming from the fall in Genesis 3, a man looks to Eve for validation. A woman can easily become man's source of worth and value. When given the power to validate, a wife is equally given the power to devalue. Woman cannot validate man. This is something only God can provide for a man. You must look to God to father you, validate you, heal you, and empower you.

2. Know her story. To fight for and shepherd a woman's heart, a man must know her story. How much of her story do you know? Do you know the intricacies of her early years? What hurts and wounds does she carry? What is her relationship with her dad like? And mom? What about her dreams and desires? There is no formula for loving a woman. Spend time getting to know her story, not just the facts but also what lies beneath the facts.

3. Fight for her. There is a battle taking place, which means she has an enemy. Satan has a target on the heart of your woman. She bears God's image in her beauty, strength, vulnerability, and mercy. And the villain hates her for it. Instead of fighting her, you must battle with her against the enemy. Based on her story, what are the specific ways she has been opposed: comparison, self-image, wounds, doubt, fear, etc.?

4. Shepherd her. If the battle calls forth the warrior, then shepherding calls forth the lover/shepherd in a man. Every woman carries wounds, hurts, and struggles. As trust is earned, a man is able to extend the mercies of God toward her wounded, sometimes fearful heart. God alone can heal and strengthen her, but you can pave the way for that to happen.

5. Romance her. In the dating phase, a man pursues and romances. He goes out of his way to make her feel special. Once married, there is a tendency for romance to be replaced with work, paying bills, raising children, and completing household projects. Romance, though sometimes spontaneous, is most often a choice. Plan date nights. Plan a weekend getaway. Surprise her with a favorite gift or treat. To know that you are thinking of her will do wonders for her heart.

6. Talk to her. Most men are doers more than talkers. Men want a task to complete or a project to manage. But a woman's heart cannot be treated like a project or to-do list. Talking involves both listening and sharing. Listen to her without distractions or an agenda. Look her in the eyes when she is talking. Instead of shutting down, share about your day, your frustrations, and your hopes. Model honesty and transparency in the marriage.

7. Know her core fears. Insecurity, fear, and anxiety are lifelong companions for a woman. Some women compensate through drivenness and control while others retreat and hide relationally. What are you wife's core fears? How does she feel "not enough" in your marriage? How does she feel like "too much" in your marriage? Fear can be a ploy of Satan to defeat your wife and diminish her faith in God. Know her fears and commit to walk with her to overcome them.

8. Become the spiritual leader of your home. Most men hear that statement and feel overwhelmed. To be a spiritual leader sounds

like achieving supersaint status. Nothing could be further from the truth. A spiritual leader is the chief servant in the home. He thinks about others before himself. He models brokenness and honesty. He admits his wrongs. And he encourages family members to trust God. Do not think of spiritual leadership as perfection or sainthood. Think of it as living a life of honesty, dependence on God, and humility

Brothers, I must admit, this is difficult stuff. I feel I have failed in so many ways over the years. There is a part of me that says this is way too hard, and I just can't do it. Without the validation and life of God, I cannot. Without His fathering of me, I will only bring her my needy heart. With God's strength and guidance, we can bring her a full, validated heart. We can love her well. Consider the following list, also from *30 Days of Hope for Hurting Marriages*. Read it over and study it. We are in this together, and we can honor God in the ways we love the woman in our lives.

Here are some desires my wife and I have heard from wives over the years:

I want to be known.

Instead of fixing me, I'd rather have a listening ear.

I want to feel special.

I need to "see" your love.

Defend me and take up for me.

Be interested in my past—thoughts, dreams, doubts, and fears.

Keep your word. Follow through on what you said you would do.

A loud and abrasive tone shuts me down.

Pursue me in nonsexual ways.

Know my passions and my goals for life.

I want you to be the first to say, "Let's pray about that."

Verbal praise makes me feel loved.

Simple affection in public, like holding hands or putting your arm around me.

If I don't feel like you know or care for me, I am not going to open up sexually.

Romance me and flirt with me.

I love dates, especially when you handle the details.

Small gifts, particularly on "non-holidays."

Initiate spiritual conversations.

I want you to be a warrior and a lover.

I want to fight against the enemy with you, so include me in your prayers and Bible study.

I want to feel treasured.

Communication is very important to me.

I want to matter to you.

Help me experience alone time—time just for me.

Let's talk about our walks with God.

Lead our family toward a deeper walk with God.

I want to feel special and loved deeply.

Pray for me, and let me know that you are.

I want to feel secure and stable in our relationship.

ABOUT THE AUTHOR

Dr. Randy Hemphill is passionate about leading people to find freedom in Christ. Through years of pastoring, counseling, and teaching, he has witnessed the transformation that comes when a person submits to the journey of doing important internal work. His hope for *The Restored Man* is that men would recognize the depths of their brokenness in order to more fully understand and experience the lavishness of God's grace. Randy has a deep love and appreciation for the local church and hopes this resource will create a domino effect, where healthy men make for healthy families, and ultimately healthy churches.

Randy received his bachelor's degree in religion and Christian ministries from Campbell University (1996). He then attended Beeson Divinity School of Samford University where he received his master of divinity (2001) and doctorate of ministry (2014). Randy and his wife Melody have three sons and one daughter. They reside in Birmingham, Alabama, where Randy is the founder and executive director of LIFE Ministries in addition to serving as an adjunct professor for Point University and Southeastern University.

Randy is coauthor of the devotional book, *30 Days of Hope for Hurting Marriages*.

Connect with Randy on Facebook, LinkedIn, Instagram, and Twitter (@morelifenow). You can also find information at www.lifeministriesnow.com and www.therestoredman.com.

If you enjoyed this book, will you consider sharing the message with others?

Let us know your thoughts at info@ironstreammedia.com. You can also let the author know by visiting or sharing a photo of the cover on our social media pages or leaving a review at a retailer's site. All of it helps us get the message out!

Facebook.com/IronStreamMedia

Iron Stream Books is an imprint of Iron Stream Media, which derives its name from Proverbs 27:17, "As iron sharpens iron, so one person sharpens another."

This sharpening describes the process of discipleship, one to another. With this in mind, Iron Stream Media provides a variety of solutions for churches, missionaries, and nonprofits ranging from in-depth Bible study curriculum and Christian book publishing to custom publishing and consultative services. Through our popular Life Bible Study, Student Life Bible Study brands, and New Hope imprints, ISM provides web-based full-year and short-term Bible study teaching plans as well as printed devotionals, Bibles, and discipleship curriculum.

For more information on ISM and Iron Stream Books, please visit

IronStreamMedia.com

ALSO BY
Randy Hemphill

GIFTS OF HOPE SERIES

GIFTS OF HOPE SERIES

30 DAYS OF HOPE
FOR HURTING MARRIAGES

RANDY AND MELODY HEMPHILL

RITE of PASSAGE
The Making of a Godly Man

ERIC BALLARD